Glass
of the '20s & '30s
A Collector's Guide

D1512142

MILLER'S

Glass
of the '20s & '30s

A Collector's Guide

Frankie Leibe

Special Consultant:
Jeanette Hayhurst

MILLER'S GLASS OF THE '20S & '30S: A COLLECTOR'S GUIDE
by Frankie Leibe
Special consultant: Jeanette Hayhurst

First published in Great Britain in 1999 by Miller's, a division of
Mitchell Beazley, imprints of Octopus Publishing Group Ltd,
Michelin House, 81 Fulham Road, London SW3 6RB

First published in the USA in 1999
Copyright © Octopus Publishing Group Ltd
Miller's is a registered trademark of Octopus Publishing Group Ltd
This edition distributed in the USA by Antique Collectors' Club Ltd.,
Market Street Industrial Park, Wappingers' Falls, New York, NY 12590, USA

Executive Editor **Alison Starling**
Executive Art Editor **Vivienne Brar**
Project Editor **Elisabeth Faber**
Assistant Editor **Clare Peel**
Designers **Louise Griffiths & Adrian Morris**
Illustrator **Amanda Patton**
Indexer **Sue Farr**
Production **Rachel Staveley**
Specially commissioned photography by **Premier Photography**
Jacket photography by **Steve Tanner**

ISBN 1 84000 163 1
A CIP catalog record for this book is available from the British Library
Set in Bembo, Frutiger and Shannon
Color reproduction by Vimnice Printing Press Co. Ltd., Hong Kong
Produced by Toppan Printing Co., (HK) Ltd.
Printed and bound in China
Jacket (left to right): champagne/cocktail glass by Daum, 1930s; trailed vase
by Whitefriars, 1935; engraved vase by Walsh, 1930s; molded opalescent
vase by Jobling, c.1934; "rainbow" posy vase by Royal Brierley, 1930s

contents

Where to start

Trends in collecting glass tend to be some five years behind those in ceramics, so, although the ceramics of the 1920s and 1930s were being rediscovered in the late 1960s and early 1970s, it was not until the mid- to late-1970s that the glass of the inter-war years began to be explored. What collectors discovered was a wide range of glass, much of it in traditional and historical styles, together with pieces by designers who used and revived traditional glassmaking techniques such as acid-etching, enameling, *pâte-de-verre*, molding, and pressing to create the new Art Deco styles and motifs inspired by an era of hedonism, glamor, speed, and travel.

This book is a good, accessible introduction to the glass that was produced in quantity throughout Europe, Scandinavia, and the USA in the 1920s and 1930s. As a novice collector, you can use it to gain a broad overview of the subject, perhaps before trying to narrow the field by focusing on a particular collecting theme such as technique, type, country, factory, style – whether traditional, historical, or Art Deco, or that of a particular designer – that you can explore in more depth with the help of the books listed in *What to read* (see pp.62–3).

Unmarked and unattributed glass is modestly priced and readily available, but if your first piece can be attributed to either a factory or a designer, this will provide a starting-point from which you can build up your knowledge by reading in your local library, researching in museums, visiting vetted fairs, and, above all, handling glass. A reputable dealer is an essential part of this process. He or she can supply information, answer questions, provide an opportunity to handle pieces, and – most importantly – build up a good long-term relationship that is mutually beneficial. Do not feel that you have to buy every time you visit; never be afraid to ask the price, and do not be afraid to say if you cannot afford a piece – many dealers take credit cards or are prepared to make arrangements for payments in stages. Do buy what you like and the very best you can afford. A $100 piece once a month may well become a $200 piece every two months, as your knowledge and tastes develop.

As your collection grows (as it inevitably will) you will need to decide how to show it off. A display cabinet (especially one that is Art Deco in style) is ideal and solves the problem of dusting; glass shelving in alcoves with down lighting is an alternative, but pieces will need to be cleaned with an anti-static duster; frosted bathroom windows can often provide a perfect background for transparent colored glass. If you are displaying heavy items, 8mm (⅓in) or 10mm (⅜in) shelves will be needed rather than the standard 6mm (¼in). Pieces that are not on display should be stored in bubble wrap or newspaper in a cool dry place; warmth and damp are a dangerous combination when storing glass, as print from damp newspaper will transfer to the surface of the glass. Glass can withstand extremes of temperature but not sudden changes of heat. Wash pieces in tepid soapy water, or clean with a spray-on glass cleaner, and finish with a paper kitchen towel. Dishwashers and glass are not compatible; the water is far too hot and bakes any limescale onto the surface of the glass.

Vulnerability will be an important consideration, as glass is very easy to break. A compromise on insurance is a false economy, so if possible insure your collection separately. Photograph your pieces and keep detailed records of what you bought, the place and date of purchase, the price paid and condition each piece was in, together with the descriptive receipts that a good dealer will provide.

Good condition is most important. Check for damage or restoration by feeling, looking, and asking. If a perfect example of a particular technique or form is outside your price range, a damaged affordable piece may be better than no example at all and will certainly be a useful learning aid. Prices for glass vary greatly, but, apart from such notable exceptions as pieces by Lalique or Gallé, in general 1920s and 1930s glass is modestly priced; it is important to remember that a piece does not have to be highly priced to be good. Buy what you like, buy the best example you can afford, and if and when you no longer like it, sell it and trade up. Never abandon hope – if the piece you set your heart on has been sold, you were probably not meant to have it in the first place. The agonies you experience over the pieces you cannot buy will soon be replaced by the ecstasies you feel over the pieces you can.

Prices and dimensions

Prices for antiques vary, depending on the condition of the item, geographical location, and market trends, so the price ranges given throughout this book should be seen as guides to value only.

Abbreviations used for dimensions are as follows: **ht** height; **diam.** diameter; **l.** length. Dimensions are given in both centimeters and inches.
Conversion rate: $1.65 = £1.00.

Blown glass

Blowing is one of the earliest and simplest glassmaking techniques. The glassblower collects a gather of molten glass on the end of the blowing iron and blows it to the desired size by either free-blowing or blowing into a mold, continuously spinning the glass to create an even surface. The glass is then transferred to a solid rod, known as a "pontil iron", for shaping. When the required shape and size are achieved, the piece is removed from the rod and allowed to cool slowly. In the 1920s and 1930s the technique was an integral part of the return to good simple form that was a basic tenet of the Modernist architects. Swedish glassmakers and such architect-designers as British-based Keith Murray used the malleable nature of glass to produce bold, contemporary shapes that are now highly collectible.

▼ **Vase by Murray**
New Zealand-born architect Keith Murray was employed from 1932 as a freelance designer at the firm of Stevens & Williams, of Brierley Hill, near Stourbridge. The bold modern form of this simple free-blown vase with a rim flared with tools clearly shows the influence of Murray's architectural training. Overall symmetry, a smooth surface, and impeccable blowing are all essential with such minimalist pieces, which are increasingly sought after. Although marks are often difficult to decipher, this vase is acid-etched with the "Keith Murray" signature and the words "Royal Brierley".

Vase by Murray, 1930s, ht 19cm/7in, **$330–495**

▶ **Vase by Murray**
This large free-blown pale blue vase, also designed by Murray, features spotted decoration created by small pockets of air. The gather of glass was slightly expanded by blowing and then dipped into a mold with indentations; it was cooled slightly before being covered with another layer of hot glass, which because of the temperature difference did not flow into the indentations. The Keith Murray mark on the base is very indistinct, but the form is clearly identified as number 307A in the catalog of Murray patterns.

Vase by Murray, 1934/5, ht 31cm/12in, **$577–742**

Ice-glass bowl, 1920s, ht 7.5cm/3in, **$66–99**

Vase by Orrefors, 1932, ht 17.5cm/6¾in, **$132–198**

▲ Vase by Orrefors

Optical blowing, where a design exploits the refractive and reflective qualities of glass as shown above, is synonymous with the Swedish companies Orrefors and Kosta. The gather of glass was slightly blown, marked with parallel horizontal indentations using glass tweezers, and blown to full size. The smooth outer surface was created by rolling the vase in a damp wood former. Here, the pale blue colour adds to the rippling effect. The base is marked with the factory name and pattern number.

▲ Ice-glass bowl

The crackled effect seen on this unmarked bowl was achieved by dipping the blown bubble of molten glass into cold water. The piece was then completely reheated and expanded, so that the cracks widened and fused back into the molten glass. The iridescence is closely associated with a type of brightly colored pressed glass, known as "Carnival" glass, made in large quantities in the USA. Such pieces are found in many colours including "gold", "blue", and "green"; the shiny finish is typical of "Carnival" glass. The modest price of this piece makes it an ideal starting-point for a novice collector.

Vase by Schneider, 1925, ht 19cm/7in, **$330–495**

▼ Vase by Schneider

Another variation on free-blowing was used by the French firm of Schneider to produce this bubbly vase. The gather of clear glass was rolled on the marver into a mixture of crushed glass, grains of color, and a soda-based substance. The gather was then coated with another layer of clear glass and expanded, so that the soda-based substance produced random air bubbles in the glass. The black foot – a characteristic feature of Schneider glass – was added separately.

Optic molding

Many designs in the 1920s and 1930s capitalized on the intrinsic reflective and refractive qualities of glass, in particular the way in which it could be blown into a ribbed mold and then expanded to emulate the rippling effect of waves. Most British makers – including Whitefriars Glassworks, Thomas Webb & Sons, and John Walsh Walsh – produced ranges that exploited this quality, and further heightened it by the use of watery colors, especially soft blues, greens, and ambers. Often part of popular, mass-produced ranges, many such pieces were unsigned; however, they can be identified by the colors and wave patterns associated with individual factories.

Vase by Whitefriars, 1920s and 1930s, ht 31cm/12in, **$297–363**

► Vase by Whitefriars Glassworks

The wave-like effect on this vase was created by free-blowing the glass into a horizontally ribbed mold, and then into a vertically ribbed mold. Introduced in the 1920s, this design was produced until the end of the 1930s. It was made in three sizes, of which the largest, shown here, is the rarest and most valuable, and in several colors – "sapphire blue" (rarest), "sky blue" (shown here), "yellow", "green", and "red". This pattern was also used on bowls and lamp-bases and was part of a commercially very successful range that is still easily found.

Vase by Webb, 1930s, ht 25cm/9¾in, **$132–198**

▼ Vase by Thomas Webb & Sons

Wave patterns were popular with all the major glass manufacturers. The piece shown here was initially mold-blown to create the continous wave pattern, with the pattern on the glass becoming increasingly elongated toward the bottom of the piece. Webb's colors were more acidic than the softer, more watery ones used by Whitefriars. Amethyst-colored pieces are in general the rarest and most highly priced, as they fit into what is now a niche collecting area. This example is marked "Thomas Webb".

▼ Decanter by Thomas Webb & Sons

Decanters were usually accompanied by matching glasses. Complete sets are rarely found today, and decanters are highly collectable on their own. The design shown below was mold-blown and then hand-blown; hand-blowing enlarged the piece and expanded the pattern. The colored stopper was mold-blown to size, so the pattern on it remains crisp, and the mold lines, which can no longer be seen on the decanter, are still clear. The colored foot was applied separately. "Amethyst" decanters are more popular than green- or yellow-colored ones.

▼ Vase by Whitefriars Glassworks

The shape of this vase, and its diamond-molded pattern, were inspired by shards found at a dig at Woodchester Glasshouse, in Gloucestershire, which had been operating in the late 16th and early 17thC. Diamond molding had also been used by early Venetian glassmakers, and in the 1930s many British companies, including Whitefriars Glassworks, reintroduced the technique. These vases were made in various colors including "sapphire", "gold amber", "green", "sky blue" (shown here), and, most sought after, "sanctuary blue".

Vase by Whitefriars, 1930s, ht 15cm/6in, **$132–198**

- Optic molding was used by a range of manufacturers, although subtle differences in style and color help to identify unmarked wares.
- These ranges were very popular and produced in large quantities. As they are readily found, good condition is important; minor surface scratches only will be acceptable.
- "Amethyst" is now a collecting niche; other popular colors include "sanctuary blue" by Whitefriars Glassworks.

▼ Decanter by John Walsh Walsh

Wrythen ribbing was another old Venetian technique revived by Whitefriars Glassworks at the end of the 19thC and popular in the 1920s and 1930s. This decanter has been dipped into a mold and then hand-finished to produce squared-off, dimpled sides. It is part of the "Old Venetian Suite" in the Walsh catalogue of 1929, but these ribbed, dimpled tablewares were so popular that they were made by most major manufacturers. Most are unmarked and relatively affordable.

Decanter by Walsh, 1929, ht 27.5cm/ 10¾in, **$165–198**

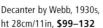

Decanter by Webb, 1930s, ht 28cm/11in, **$99–132**

Studio glass

Before 1920 there was a clear distinction between glass designer and glassmaker. One of the first to combine the two roles was Maurice Marinot, a French painter and sculptor who began experimenting with glass in 1911 and in 1913 exhibited glass he had designed and produced himself. A fellow Frenchman, Henri Navarre, inspired by Marinot's work, began to produce studio glass in 1924, and was joined by André Thuret, who went on to work alone at the Alfortville Glassworks near Paris. The one-off luxury pieces produced by these artist–craftsmen are rare, very sought after, and correspondingly highly priced; they represent the pinnacle of blown-glass design, and prices reflect their exclusivity and their technical difficulty.

◀ **Perfume bottle by Marinot**

The thick glass and internal bubbly decoration of this blown perfume bottle may well have inspired the cased bubbly glass widely produced by British manufacturers (see pp.16–19). This bottle is a classic example of Marinot's range of small, simple forms with tiny clear-glass stoppers, and also features his characteristic profusion of air bubbles. It is marked with Marinot's etched signature, together with a paper label numbered "849", referring to the inventory drawn up by his daughter Florence (the only archive material to have survived the bombing of Marinot's workshop in World War II).

Perfume bottle by Marinot, 1924, ht 12.5cm/5in, **$4,950– 8,250**

◀ **Perfume bottle by Marinot**

The time and effort expended by Marinot on his glass explains its rarity and high value. This red perfume bottle (inventory number 1808) took over a year to make, being blown, cased in clear glass, and, over time, repeatedly dipped in hydrofluoric acid to produce the highly controlled, deeply etched decoration. Such exclusive one-off pieces were status symbols in their day, and they remain extremely rare and correspondingly valuable.

Perfume bottle by Marinot, mid-1920s, ht 11.5cm/ 4½in, **$24,750– 33,000**

Vase by Navarre, c.1927,
ht 12.5cm/4⅞in, **$1,320–1,980**

▼ **Bowl by Marinot**
Although classed as a
bowl, the design shown below
is primarily a piece of
sculpture. It is one of the few
larger pieces produced by
Marinot, probably because
such a heavy item would have
been extremely difficult to
support during production.
Marinot has combined great
technical and imaginative skill
to create a sophisticated piece
of artistic, colorless, bubbly
glass, and this is reflected in
its high value. The piece is
signed and has the inventory
number 1808.

▲ **Vase by Navarre**
Navarre, who trained as an
architect and a sculptor, began
to experiment with glass in
1924 and from c.1930 was
making simple pieces with
thick, heavy walls and colored
internal decoration. His designs
are almost as rare and valuable
as those by Marinot (by whom
he was inspired).

▼ **Perfume bottle by Thuret**
Thuret's work is either free-
blown (as in this case) or
mold-blown. The technique of
sandwiching a layer of colored
glass between two layers of
clear glass demanded great
technical expertise; if
misjudged the colored layers
would splinter, rather like a
car windscreen. Most pieces
are signed "André Thuret".

Bowl by Marinot, 1929, ht
10.5cm/4in, **$6,600–9,900**

Perfume bottle by Thuret,
c.1930, ht 21.5cm/8½in,
$3,300–4,950

Major European cased glass

Cased glass is composed of two or more blown layers of differently colored glass, one of which is often clear. The technique can be combined with trailing, cutting, engraving, acid-etching, and trapped air bubbles to produce highly decorative designs. In the 1920s and 1930s the Loetz glassworks in Vienna produced a range of extremely collectable and very influential cased glass in bold Art Deco forms and bright, contrasting colors. In Sweden master craftsmen at the Orrefors and Kosta glassworks developed the "Graal" and "Ariel" ranges that are now recognized as the early masterpieces of cased glass; such wares are very highly priced, compared with pieces of the same design manufactured after World War II.

Vase by Loetz, early
1920s, ht 30cm/9¾in,
$1,320–1,980

▶ **Vase by Loetz**
The bold, simple form, strong contrasting colors, and high-quality glass seen on this vase are hallmarks of a range of simple cased glass made by Loetz in the 1920s. An orange gather of glass was rolled on the marver to collect the black canes that form the decoration, and the gather was then cased in clear glass and blown to size and shape. In general, larger and more complex forms are more highly priced than smaller, simpler pieces. Although unsigned, Loetz designs can be identified from factory records.

Loetz-style vase,
1930s, ht 21cm/8in,
$82–247

▼ **Loetz-style vase**
With its bold design and strong contrasting colors this simple cased vase from Czechoslovakia (now the Czech Republic) could well be mistaken for a piece by Loetz. The technique used to produce it was very similar to that used to produce the genuine Loetz piece shown left, although the decoration was made by drawing the black glass up the vase rather than rolling it. The clue to the origins of this piece lies in the finishing – the flat-cut top lacks the smooth rounded edge of the real Loetz piece. Nevertheless this remains a good example, very much in the style of the period, and without doubt more affordable than a vase by Loetz.

"Graal" bowl,
1975, diam.
18cm/7in,
$495–660

▼ Vase by Loetz
This stylish vase has been made extra glamorous by the addition of iridescence and a crackled effect to the first layer of pink glass (also cased in clear glass). The charming black bun feet would have been added at a later stage. This piece may well have been designed by one of the distinguished designers of the Wiener Werkstätte ("Vienna Workshops") such as Josef Hoffman, Otto Prutscher, or Michael Powolny, all of whom designed glass for the company, although their pieces are unsigned.

▲ "Graal" bowl
"Graal" glass was developed for Orrefors in 1916 by the designer Simon Gate with the master glassblower Knut Bergkvist. The complex technique involves casing a gather of clear glass in a layer of glass of another color, expanding it to a bubble, cooling it until cold, engraving or cutting away the top color to form the decoration, reheating the glass, casing it in clear glass, and then expanding it to the desired shape. Such pieces demanded supreme craftsmanship and were very costly to make. This bowl is signed "Orrefors S. Graal nr.1924 E.5. Edvard Hald" – "Hald" is the name of the designer.

Vase by Loetz,
c.1920, ht
22.5cm/8¾in,
$1,980–2,310

▼ "Ariel" bowl
The technique for producing "Ariel" glass, developed c.1930 by Bergkvist, Edvin Öhrström, and Vicke Lindstrand, was similar to that used to make "Graal", but was employed on much thicker glass and with one or more color casings. Early "Graal" and "Ariel" pieces are prohibitively highly priced for the novice collector. Post-war pieces inspired by 1930s design, as shown here, use exactly the same technique but are far more modestly priced.

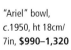

"Ariel" bowl,
c.1950, ht 18cm/
7in, **$990–1,320**

Monart cased glass

In 1924 the Moncrieff Glassworks in Perth, Scotland – until then primarily manufacturers of scientific glass – launched a new range of art glass, known as "Monart". The range was the brainchild of Mrs Moncrieff, who collaborated with the highly talented Spanish glassblower Salvador Ysart to produce a variety of clear-cased, internally decorated wares in many different colors and patterns. Some pieces reflect Mrs Moncrieff's passion for Chinese design, particularly in their oriental-inspired forms. Although scientific glass remained the firm's major output, with Monart never exceeding ten per cent of the total production, the range was manufactured from 1924 until 1961 with a break during World War II; it is avidly sought after by collectors today.

▼ **"Pull-up" vase**

Monart pieces were all produced using the same basic technique. A gather of clear glass was rolled on a marver covered with small shards of colored glass and then cased in clear glass, so that the color was sandwiched between two layers of clear glass. The pattern shown here was created using a tool to "pull up" the layer of colored glass; this produced what became a classic Monart design that was used on a wide range of different shapes. Monart wares were never signed, but were marked instead with a paper label on the base.

"Pull-up" vase, 1930s, ht 27.5cm/10¾in, **$396–462**

▶ **"Nebulae" vase**

The foot of this vase shows the dark, marvered effect produced before the molten glass was expanded by blowing to create the soft, cloudy "Nebulae" pattern. Although this color scheme was very popular, the lop-sided rim on this piece detracts from its value – had the shape been symmetrical, this vase would be worth between $528 and $627. Although all Monart colors and shapes have been recorded in company catalogs, the random element involved in free-blowing a colored piece means that no two such items are ever identical.

"Nebulae" vase, 1930s, ht 18cm/7in, **$330–412**

▼ Aventurine bowl

Large shards of glass, known as "pebbles" or "slabs", were used to create the colored pattern featured on this thick-walled glass bowl. Strong color and bold form make this piece very attractive to collectors, as do the aventurine inclusions (sparkling metallic particles), which add gold flecks to the pattern and accentuate the marble or stone effect of the thick glass and classical form.

▼ Blown bowl

The pattern on this bowl, which combines color and air bubbles, is one of the rarer Monart designs and therefore highly sought after. The powdered glass was set out in lines on the marver, and the gather of clear glass was rolled onto the powder before being dipped into a mold to produce the ribbed effect, and then cased. "Red" is the most sought-after color but is comparatively rare as it is a difficult color to produce.

Blown bowl, 1930s, ht 10cm/4in, **$660–825**

Aventurine bowl, 1930s, diam. 25.5cm/10in, **$363–462**

▼ "Paisley shawl" vase

"Paisley shawl" is another rare pattern used on Monart glass. Here, the vase has been re-marvered to create an extra layer of color and mica (a mineral giving a shiny finish), and then tooled to produce the swirling, slightly iridescent pattern. This combination of internal cased and external decoration is rare and valuable, and such colorful pieces are keenly collected. Two other highly collectable patterns that use the same technique are "Cloisonné" and "Stoneware".

"Paisley shawl" vase, 1930s, ht 24cm/10in, **$2,310–2,970**

Other British cased glass

The success of the beautiful colored-and-cased glass produced by the Moncrieff Glassworks inspired many similar ranges from a large number of other British factories. All of these companies used slightly different patterns and colors, and this helps collectors to identify unmarked pieces. Such major manufacturers as the Whitefriars Glassworks produced notable designs, including the "Cloudy" range; small family firms such as Nazeing also produced attractive pieces, and these wares are still very modestly priced, because so little is known about them. However, the company that was closest in spirit and style to Monart was the London firm of Gray-Stan, a small art-glass workshop that produced a range of well-documented, sought-after, handmade, colored-and-cased glass.

▶ **"Cloudy" vase by Whitefriars Glassworks**
Between 1928 and 1939, Whitefriars Glassworks produced a series of bowls and vases in colored glass with small air bubbles that produced a distinctive "cloudy" pattern. The bucket-shaped piece shown here is the most affordable form in the range; oriental-inspired forms are worth at least half or twice as much again. Colors included the brilliant "sanctuary blue" shown here, "green", "yellow", and "red" (rarest). Two-color combinations are very sought after. Although unmarked, the shapes, colors, and patterns are all identifiable from the firm's catalogs and archives.

"Cloudy" vase, 1930s, ht 20cm/8in, **$297–363**

Vase by Gray-Stan, 1930s, ht 25cm/9¾in, **$297–363**

▼ **Vase by Gray-Stan**
In 1926 Mrs Graydon-Stannus launched Gray-Stan art glass from her Battersea factory. Although many forms, including the classic, elegant, Chinese-style vase shown here, are reminiscent of Monart, Gray-Stan pieces have a much more powdery finish and use a different color palette. Gray-Stan wares, made until 1936, must be signed for premium value, although the large number of unsigned pieces can be identified from existing signed pieces.

• Pieces by Whitefriars Glassworks are very sought after. Unlike wares by less well-known firms such as Nazeing, Whitefriars glass is rarely misattributed because of extensive company catalogs.

• Pieces by less well-documented companies are more modestly priced and provide a good starting-point for novice collectors.

• Vases have often been used, and collectors should check for limescale deposit by feeling the insides for rough texture.

Vase by Gray-Stan, 1930s,
ht 25cm/9¾in, **$660–742**

▲ Vase by Gray-Stan

The characteristic swirling, powdery Gray-Stan pattern is seen here in "red" – a rare and sought-after color that was unstable when heated and inherently difficult to produce. The dimpled sides are reminiscent of successful designs by Whitefriars Glassworks and John Walsh Walsh, and were very popular in the 1930s. A combination of large size, rare color, and the Gray-Stan signature in script explain the high value of this piece.

Vase by Nazeing, 1930s,
ht 23cm/9in, **$165–231**

▲ Vase by Nazeing

Little is known about the Nazeing glass produced in the 1930s, as there are no company archives for that period. Extensive handling of items known to have been supplied to retailers by Nazeing is therefore the most reliable form of attribution. This piece features the characteristic "cloudy" pattern dotted with tiny bubbles that is a reliable identifying feature of glass by this firm.

▼ Vase by Nazeing

Although this amethyst-colored vase is similar to some Monart shapes, the over-large foot and wide, flaring rim combined with the distinctive "cloudy" pattern identify it as Nazeing glass. This is a very attractive piece and a good starting-point for a novice collector as it is relatively affordable. Many Nazeing pieces are modestly priced at present because comparatively little is known about the firm's Art Deco production. With all pieces, check carefully for chips or blemishes to what should be a smooth uniform surface.

Vase by Nazeing, 1930s,
ht 18cm/7in, **$132–198**

Other cased glass

Bubbly, marvered cased glass was also very popular in Europe, and the wide range of wares produced offers great scope to collectors. Among the leading exponents in France was Schneider, whose vases and bowls were celebrated at the 1925 Paris Exposition Internationale des Arts Décoratifs et Industriels Modernes ("International Exhibition of Decorative and Modern Industrial Arts"). Glassworks in Czechoslovakia (now the Czech Republic) also made cased glass, although their pieces tend to fall into two distinct categories: a high-quality range comparable to good French and British pieces, and less-inspired, very commercial glass. In Germany the Württemberg Metalwork Factory ("WMF"), although better known for Art Nouveau metalwork, produced some art glass, notably pieces by such top freelance designers as Wilhelm Wagenfeld. In The Netherlands the Leerdam factory also owed much of its success to talented designers, among them Andries Dirk Copier.

▼ **"Jades" vase by Schneider**
The elegant, elongated form of this pebble-marvered, blown "Jades" vase is typical of Schneider, as are the stoneware effect and applied dark-red handles. However, the satin-mat finish is rare and was probably created by sandblasting the glass and then polishing it with a weak acid. This design was produced in quantity and is readily available, unlike the vase shown right. The piece on the left is signed "Schneider" in script; the company name is sometimes found in block capitals, and some pieces are also marked "Le Verre Français".

"Jades" vase, 1920s,
ht 30cm/11¾in, **$660–825**

▶ **Vase by Schneider**
A more refined version of the vase shown left can be seen in the rare piece shown right. Here the applied handles have been extended into elegant tears, and the typical black foot has become part of an archetypally bold Art Deco color combination – red with a white cased body decorated with internal bubbles. The engraved company mark is clearly visible.

Vase by Schneider, 1925, ht
18cm/7in, **$3,300–4,950**

Bowl by WMF, c.1933, diam. 25.5cm/10in, **$115–148**

▲ Bowl by WMF

This blown bowl combines several decorative techniques. Strips of colored glass were rolled on a marver onto a clear gather of glass, which was then ribbed in a mold before being plunged into cold water to create the crackled effect. The piece would then have been reheated and expanded to enhance the ribbed design and bring out the flame-like strips of color and the crackled effect. This combination of effects is thought to be exclusive to WMF, whose pieces are often unsigned.

▼ Lamp-base

This mold-blown, cased, bubbly-glass lamp-base was manufactured by an unknown factory in Czechoslovakia, and would originally have been worth little more than $66 to $99. A number of very similar pieces have been found complete with paper labels identifying the factory, which may well have supplied many different retail outlets. With the presence of such labels and attribution possible, the value of the piece has trebled.

Lamp-base, 1930s, ht 20cm/8in, **$247–297**

▼ "Serica" vase by Leerdam

In 1923 Copier joined Leerdam as principal designer, and was responsible for two of their studio ranges: "Unica", which consisted of one-off pieces only, and "Serica", a series of limited-edition vases, with characteristic thick walls and internal decoration of bubbles or "seaweed" patterns. Leerdam Art Deco pieces are rare and are as highly priced today as they were in the 1920s. Most pieces in the "Unica" and "Serica" ranges are marked with the name of the factory, the designer, and the series. This example is marked "SERICA COPIER".

"Serica" vase by Leerdam, 1927, ht 20cm/8in, **$495–660**

Iridescent glass

Inspired by excavations of Roman glass with an iridescent finish caused by a reaction with metal oxides during burial, in 1878 the British firm of Thomas Webb & Sons patented a process for iridizing contemporary glass by exposing it to fumes of metal oxides. The technique, which subsequently involved painting or spraying glass with lustrous colors that became shiny when heated, was developed and refined in Vienna by Loetz and in the USA by Louis Comfort Tiffany. Loetz and Tiffany glass are keenly collected and valuable; iridescent glass by other manufacturers is more modestly priced and readily found. In the 1920s and 1930s iridescent glass was closely associated with Art Nouveau; it tended to wane in popularity with the emergence of bubbly cased glass.

▶ **"Amethyst" vase**
Although unmarked, this "amethyst" vase with silvered spots and a crimped top was almost certainly made in Bohemia (now part of the Czech Republic), as the form is typical of many wares in 19thC British styles made in Bohemia and imported into Britain after World War I. This example was hand-blown and then put into a fume chamber before being finished, and the iridescence is only found on the outside. This vase is a good example of fine quality glass that will be very modestly priced because it is as yet unattributable.

"Amethyst" vase, 1920s, ht 13cm/5in, **$132–198**

▼ **"Fan" vase by John Walsh Walsh**
All-over iridescence, as seen on this blown-and-thrown opalescent vase, is achieved by iridizing after finishing. This shape is very fragile – few examples have survived, and those that have must be in tip-top condition for maximum value. This design was made in several colors: "green" is rarest, "flint" the most commonly found and affordable, and "straw opal", which shows off the typical Walsh mother-of-pearl iridescence to best effect, the most desirable and highly priced. All pieces by this British firm are much more affordable than equivalent pieces made in continental Europe.

"Fan" vase by Walsh, 1900, ht 24cm/9 ½in, **$495–660**

▼ Vase by Loetz

Loetz is closely associated with iridescent designs with a characteristic oil-on-water effect, as shown on the free-blown piece below; the blue of this example is also typical. However, the combination of iridescent and plain glass – a technically difficult two-tone effect, which is correspondingly highly priced – is fairly unusual. Dating can be problematic, as production of iridescent glass by Loetz began before World War I and continued into the 1920s.

Vase by Loetz, c.1921, ht 19.5cm/7¾in, **$660–990**

"Cypriote" vase by Tiffany, c.1920, ht 18cm/7in, **$3,300–4,950**

▲ "Cypriote" vase by Tiffany Studios

The name of Tiffany is virtually synonymous with highly stylized, beautifully finished iridescent Art Nouveau glass. However, the company also produced a range known as "Cypriote" in free-blown, organic shapes with a pitted iridescent surface that resembled the decayed and corroded finish found on ancient glass. All Tiffany pieces are signed, and this vase bears the company name on the base, together with the letter "P", indicating a date of c.1921.

"Gladioli" vase by Tiffany, c.1920, ht 26.5cm/10½in, **$8,250–11,550**

- Iridescent glass is now produced in large quantities by studio glassmakers worldwide, and it has been known for work by contemporary American and British artists to be sold as early iridescent glass.
- The best safeguard is to buy from a reputable dealer and ask for a detailed receipt.
- Pieces by Loetz have been widely copied, so collectors should be particularly cautious of all designs with Loetz-style iridescence.

▼ "Gladioli" vase by Tiffany Studios

This vase has been decorated using two iridizing techniques. Metal oxides were painted onto the hot glass to create the floral decoration, and the piece was then exposed to a single vapor to give an overall iridescence. Tiffany pieces such as the example shown proved very inspirational to the American firm of Quezal, and although glass by Quezal is usually signed with the company name, it is occasionally found with a spurious Tiffany signature. Novice collectors should seek professional advice if in any doubt over the authenticity.

Applied decoration

Early (15thC) Venetian glassmakers were supreme exponents of applied decoration – the addition of trailed molten glass to a hot glass form, so that when the piece cools, the applied decoration stands proud. Such decoration, although extremely vulnerable, was newly popular in the 19thC, and in the 1920s and 1930s many designs in historical and traditional styles were produced alongside a variety of wares in bold modern styles. Italian glassmakers perpetuated the historical tradition, and in perfect condition their pieces can be very valuable. British factories such as the Whitefriars Glassworks produced both traditional and modern ranges; their pieces in bold Art Deco shapes with trailed decoration are generally more affordable than the glass in historical styles.

Ribbon-trailed vase by Whitefriars, 1935, ht 18cm/7in, **$297–363** (single color **$80–115)**

▼ **Ribbon-trailed vase by Whitefriars Glassworks**
Barnaby Powell designed this hand-blown, ribbon-trailed vase for Whitefriars Glassworks in 1935. Its pattern number was 9030, and the two-color version was produced until 1949. The most commonly found two color-version is "blue" over "sea green", but "amethyst" over "blue" is also known; two-color versions are rarer and more desirable than the more commonly found one-color versions, which were produced until 1964. Each vase is unique because the trailed decoration, which was applied at the top of the vase and then pulled down, differs slightly from piece to piece.

▶ **"Strap" vase**
This "sky blue" vase with "amethyst" applied decoration was also designed by Powell. The decoration was formed by applying a separately blown bubble to the free-blown body and then pulling the bubble down to flatten it. The clear "eye" at the center of the tear shows where the bubble was blown onto the glass. This piece is rare, and the color scheme shown is the only one known. A similar technique was used by the designer Geoffrey Baxter from 1969 until 1971, but in different colors and forms; check the Whitefriars catalog to avoid confusion.

"Strap" vase, 1934, ht 18cm/7in, **$577–742**

Venetian vase, late 1920s,
ht 22cm/8¾in, **$49–66**

▲ Venetian vase

The traditional Venetian shape of this free-blown vase is offset by several features that give the piece a distinctly Art Deco feel; most notable are the stylish combination of pinkish glass with black decoration, the eye-catching design and bold application of the nipped swag decoration, and the subtle use of iridescence, probably by spraying. In perfect condition, such a rare piece would command between $495 and $660. However, as a piece of trailing is missing from this example, and this cannot be fully restored (hot glass cannot be applied to cold), the value of the vase is very dramatically reduced.

▼ Threaded bowl

Although designed in the 1920s, the threaded blue decoration on this flint bowl is essentially Victorian rather than Art Deco. The blue glass was thinly trailed onto the hand-blown flint body, starting at the rim where the trail is thicker and darker. The body was then dipped into a ribbed mold, and the thick bun foot, which also has trailing to the underside, was flattened on a wooden board. Other color schemes known include "red" on "red" (rarest and most valuable), "yellow" on "yellow", and "green" on "green". Designed by William Butler for Whitefriars Glassworks, this vase was produced in five sizes, the smallest of which is shown here.

Threaded bowl, 1920s,
ht 10cm/4in, **$132–198**

Römer by Whitefriars, 1931, ht 14.5cm/ 5¾in, **$660–990**

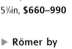

▶ Römer by Whitefriars Glassworks

This *Römer*, inspired by 17thC German drinking glasses with ovoid bowls, cylindrical stems, and flared feet, was designed by Harry Powell. Although made of crystal, this piece has been given a sea-green tinge in the style of the green *Waldglas* ("wood glass"), from which early *Römer* were made. The prunts on the stem were applied as blobs and then shaped with special tools. Very few of these glasses have survived, probably because they were costly to make and not commercially viable.

Pressed & mold-blown glass

Pressed glass is produced by pouring molten glass into a mold and then pushing it down with a plunger to create a molded exterior and a smooth, hollow interior. The technique was first developed in the 1830s in the USA as a way of mass-producing inexpensive copies of cut glass; it was revived in the 1930s and used to make colorful and now collectable Art Deco vases, figures, and trinket sets by such British companies as Jobling & Co., Bagley Crystal Co., and George Davidson & Co. With mold-blowing – a long-established technique used in the inter-war years to produce a wide range of glass from inexpensive tableware to more exclusive decorative pieces – the gather is blown into a full-size mold (usually two-piece) with deep relief decoration that can be felt on the interior of the piece.

Pressed-glass vase by Jobling, 1930s, ht 25.5cm/ 10in, **$82–115**

◀ **Pressed-glass vase by Jobling & Co.**
This vase, decorated with stylized flowers in relief, is a good example of affordable, underrated, classic Art Deco glass. Such pieces, mostly unmarked, can be researched in trade catalogs and pattern books, although attribution is not essential for full value. This vase would have been designed by an in-house designer and produced in large quantities, which makes it readily available today. Such modestly priced pieces must be in perfect condition to merit attention; always check the insides of vases for limescale build-up, as this is difficult to remove.

▼ **"Koala bear" vase by Bagley Crystal Co.**
Bagley began producing pressed glass in 1912, and by the 1920s was the leading manufacturer of inexpensive domestic pressed glass. Its reputation received a boost in 1934, when it was given the royal seal of approval from Queen Mary. This "Koala bear" vase was probably made for an exhibition or as a limited production run, and is a good example of the complex type of design that could be achieved by pressing.

"Koala bear" vase by Bagley, 1930s, ht 20.5cm/8in, **$660–990**

▼ Centerpiece vase by Jobling & Co.

This frosted, pressed-glass centerpiece, one of a range of art-glass designs inspired by Lalique and launched by the firm of Jobling & Co. in 1933, was produced in a variety of pale colors, including "grey/blue", "pink", and, "green". The three pieces that make up such a centerpiece – a bowl, rose, and figure – are rarely found in top condition, and the figure is often missing.

Centerpiece vase by Jobling, late 1930s, ht 30cm/12in, **$198–297** ($33–49 without figure)

"Cloud" vase by Davidson, c.1923, ht 25.5cm/10in, **$198–247**

▲ "Cloud" vase by George Davidson & Co.

This vase is unmarked, but the mold-blown "Cloud" design, launched in 1922, identifies it as a piece by George Davidson & Co. The swirling effect was produced by stirring the color before the glass was blown into the mold. Dating is based on color: "amber" was produced in 1922, "purple" (seen here) in 1923, "tortoiseshell" (least popular) in 1928, "green" in 1933, and "scarlet" and "orange" (rarest) in 1930 and 1934 respectively.

- Look for earlier pieces, as they are more sought after than later ones. Also look for items with crisp design – definition from the mold softens with use.
- Good condition is essential for modestly priced pieces, so avoid vases with limescale build-up.
- Pieces with a frosted finish must be in perfect condition, as chips cannot be removed without losing the frosting.
- Pressed glass is generally unmarked, but attribution is not always essential for maximum value.

▼ "Lion" vase designed by D'Avesn

The two sets of vertical lines still present on the upper part of this magnificent, high-quality vase show that it was blown into a two-piece mold. Designed by Paul D'Avesn, whose work was strongly influenced by Lalique, it features typically Art Deco stylized "lions". Such a piece easily matches the quality of glass by major French names but is much more affordable. All of D'Avesn' work is signed on the base.

"Lion" vase, c.1930, ht 21cm/8in, **$1,155–1,485**

27

Opalescent glass

Thicker areas of glass cool more slowly and retain greater opacity and color than the thinner areas, which cool more quickly and remain more transparent. Venetian glassmakers exploited this property as early as the 16thC, but in the 1920s and 1930s it was celebrated French makers such as René Lalique and Marius-Ernest Sabino who were leaders in the luxury art-glass market, and whose opalescent pieces are most highly sought after by collectors today. Many other glass manufacturers produced less ambitious ranges of opalescent glass, among them the British company Jobling & Co., and their opalescent wares will be far more readily found and modestly priced.

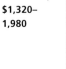

◀ **Vase by Lalique**
The name Lalique is synonymous with luxury glass, although most pieces were made by the Lalique factory rather than by the man himself. To make this vase, glass was thinly blown into an intricate bronze mold and then enameled to enhance the opalescent effect. The blue enamel shown was a particularly popular color. Fired at low temperatures, the enamel is vulnerable and needs to be checked carefully for condition; it may even be missing. Although the bronze mold could be reused many times, such pieces were very valuable then, as now, and are correspondingly rare.

Vase by
Lalique, 1920s,
ht 16cm/6in,
$1,320–1,980

▼ **"Coquilles" bowl and stand by Lalique**
The geometric shell design on this finger bowl and stand is quintessentially Art Deco. Plates and bowls were also produced, and all were press-molded to provide a smooth eating surface, with the pattern on the underneath of the piece. The plate perfectly shows how opalescent glass is cloudiest in the thicker areas – here in the thicker areas of the shells. A complete set of six finger bowls and stands would be worth at least double the value of the two pieces shown. Note the wheel-engraved signature "R. Lalique" in the center.

"Coquilles"
bowl and
stand by
Lalique,
c.1930, diam.
of stand
17cm/6¾in,
$132–165

▼ Butterfly by Sabino

Small figures and animals are now among the most popular of Sabino's range of opalescent pressed-glass wares that also included bowls, vases, trinket boxes, menu-holders, and ashtrays. The two-piece molds meant that the decoration appeared on both sides of the piece (unlike on the "Coquilles" service shown left). Many of these molds, carrying the mark "Sabino Made in France", are still in existence, and are used today to produce small birds and animals. The only way to make sure that the piece was made in the 1920s and 1930s is to check the Sabino catalog carefully to see which molds were destroyed during the war.

Butterfly by Sabino, 1930s, ht 15cm/6in, **$330–495**

▼ Bowl by Jobling & Co.

In 1933 Jobling & Co. introduced a range of pressed glass inspired by Lalique. The stylized birds on this bowl show a French influence, and the long-standing British tradition of fine mold-making can be seen in the attention to detail. This bowl is a good example of the fine pieces produced by British makers that are undervalued at present, although the situation is changing following recent exhibitions of 1920s and 1930s British glass. The design shown was registered (marked "Reg. no. 780717"), which meant that it could only be used for a limited period.

Bowl by Jobling, c.1934, diam. 18cm/7in, **$231–297**

- Opalescent glass is a popular collecting niche.
- Although Lalique is the best-known and most sought-after maker, many other pieces by lesser-known names are equally good and much more affordable.
- Later Lalique pieces from original molds may have been "aged" by the addition of an "R" to the mark.
- Condition is vital – buy nothing with a chip or crack, as opalescent glass cannot be restored to its original finish.

▼ Salt and pepper pots

These opalescent, fish-shaped salt and pepper pots with screw-on noses are typical of the small, humorous pieces produced by many factories in the north-east of England in the 1920s and 1930s. However, such items are now rare as they were often thrown away as soon as they were damaged. Today such novelty designs are very popular because they are inexpensive, easy to display, practical, and, above all, great fun. Few examples are marked.

Salt and pepper pots, 1930s, l. 5cm/2in, **$132–198** (for the pair) or **$49–66** (individually)

Pâte-de-verre

Pâte-de-verre ("glass paste") is a complex and costly technique used to create one-off and limited-edition pieces. A wax dummy of a design is enclosed in plaster, and the wax is steamed off to leave behind a plaster mold; the mold is filled with crushed glass in various colors, which is heated until it fuses, then cooled and removed from the mold. The technique, which was first used in Ancient Egypt, was rediscovered by the French sculptor Henri Cros. His experiments with powdered glass in 1884, and the discovery of the tomb of Tutankhamun in 1923, sparked a fashion for *pâte-de-verre* and Egyptian forms, a field in which French makers excelled. These French craftsmen in turn inspired Frederick Carder, one of the major names in the glassmaking world; Carder's *pâte-de-verre* pieces are even more rare and highly priced than the exclusive, experimental designs of his European counterparts.

▼ Vase by Décorchemont

François-Emile Décorchemont, a ceramicist turned glassmaker, experimented with *pâte-de-verre* as early as 1902, but it was not until after World War I that he became well known for large, thick-walled vases with surface decoration in rich, veined, streaky and bubbled colors. Typically this vase has geometric decoration on the textured exterior, and a smooth interior. From 1912 all Décorchemont wares were marked with a signature and a number.

Vase by Décorchement, 1930, ht 13cm/5in, **$4,950–8,250**

▼ Cup by Argy-Rousseau

The other leading designer of *pâte-de-verre* was Joseph-Gabriel Argy-Rousseau, also a former ceramicist. In 1921 he and a partner established Les Pâtes-de-Verres d'Argy-Rousseau, a small workshop in Paris, where they produced small, richly colored pieces. Early examples – such as this *coupe aux raisins* ("grape cup") – were decorated with the fruits, flowers, and natural motifs synonymous with Art Nouveau. Later pieces incorporated geometric designs typically associated with Art Deco.

Cup by Argy-Rousseau, 1926, ht 9cm/3in, **$2,475–3,300**

Dish by Walter,
1920s, ht 17cm/
6¾in, **$3,300–6,600**

▼ Vase by Argy-Rousseau

This vase is made of a translucent glass known as *pâte-de-cristal*. The plain form with simple geometric decoration inspired by archaic motifs is similar to pieces by Décorchemont, but can be clearly identified as Argy-Rousseau because it is more translucent, finer, and has none of the veining associated with Décorchemont's glass. This piece also has an impressed mark and can be found in the 1927 Argy-Rousseau catalog.

Vase by Argy-Rousseau,
1927, ht 13cm/5in,
$2,970–3,630

▲ Dish by Walter

The workshop established by Alméric Walter in 1919 is now best known for a range of figural and animal pieces that were produced both as individual sculptures and applied to ashtrays, paperweights, and vases. The smaller pieces have a sensuous smooth, silky finish and are relatively affordable. Walter commissioned designs from a number of artists, whose signatures often appear on their pieces, or on the maquette. The mark "A. Walter Nancy" was used from 1919.

• All [...] be ch [...] stress [...] show [...] is held [...]
• Rest[...] success[...] surface [...] worked [...] has been ...moved from the mold. Major restoration is known, especially on pieces by Argy-Rousseau, which should be checked carefully against catalog records.
• All pieces are clearly marked, and extensive archives and catalogs make identification easy.
• Fakes are not known at present, although the situation may change.

▼ Plaque by Carder

Frederick Carder was chief designer at Stevens & Williams before he moved to the USA, where from 1903 he worked for the Steuben Glassworks. He experimented with all types of glassmaking, but his *pâte-de-verre* pieces, such as this plaque, are among the rarest examples of his work. So few pieces are available on the market that it is almost impossible to assess their value.

Plaque by Carder,
c.1930s, ht 23cm/9in,
from **$8,250**

British cut glass

Although little change was made to the basic technique of cutting glass with a stone wheel, used since Roman times, by 1920 the firm of Stuart & Sons Ltd had replaced the final hand polish on its cut glass with an acid polish that gave a much brighter, shinier finish. This lustrous look was ideally suited to the bold shapes and deep, intricate, stylized cuttings that were used for abstract geometric Art Deco motifs. Although glassmakers in Bohemia (now part of the Czech Republic) were also highly skilled in making these valuable heavy Art Deco vases, bowls, and decanters, their work is now so rare as to be virtually unobtainable; instead such British firms as Thomas Webb & Sons and Stevens & Williams are at the forefront of the collecting field.

▼ Vase by Stuart & Sons Ltd

Ludwig Kny, the son of a talented Bohemian glass engraver, became chief designer at Stuart & Sons Ltd after World War I. Although, as he was a staff designer, his pieces are not always signed, they are instantly recognizable by the distinctive cutting technique, in which the outside edges of the broad cuts are then further cut with an intaglio wheel to create a brilliant refracting surface. His work, such as this hand-blown "golden amber" vase, although previously somewhat underrated, is now beginning to attract the attention it deserves.

Vase by Stuart, 1935, ht 23.5cm/9¼in, **$247–412**

▼ Bowl by Stuart & Sons Ltd

The high lead content of Stuart glass gives it a refractive and reflective quality that is ideally suited to the spectacular classic Art Deco sunburst motif featured on this rare bowl, which was also designed by Kny. Such deep and broad miter cutting would have demanded at least 4cm (1½in) of solid glass at the bottom, which would in turn have demanded an extremely strong glassblower. The company mark appears on the bottom of this piece.

Bowl by Stuart, 1935, diam. 28.5cm/11in, **$330–495**

▼ Vase by Stuart & Sons Ltd

Company records reveal that this unmarked, mold-blown vase was designed by A.R. Pearce. However, the combination of a strong form, bold design, and skilful cutting is more important than attribution. The cuts for the waves were made first and acid-polished before the stylized, three-cut, mat birds were added. The contrast between thick and thin lines in the wave-shaped cuts add to the feeling of movement, and the contrast in texture between shiny and mat glass creates a sense of depth and perspective.

Vase by Stuart, 1939, ht 20cm/8in,
$247–330

▼ Cocktail shaker by Stuart & Sons Ltd

Cocktail shakers and glasses are lasting and highly popular symbols of the hedonism of the inter-war years. Complete sets of shaker and six glasses are rare and highly priced ($1,155–1,320), but individual pieces are collectable in their own right, and single glasses are often affordable ($49–82 each). This mold-blown shaker with a fish-and-waves motif was one of the Stuart pieces made for the British Art in Industry Exhibition in 1935. It is cut in the style designed by Kny, whose mark ("L.Kny") appears on the base, together with the company name.

- British Art Deco cut glass is underrated and undervalued at present, in spite of its high quality; however, pieces by such famous artist-designers as Dame Laura Knight, Paul Nash, and Eric Ravilious command a premium, and prices for Keith Murray designs are rising.
- Typical Art Deco motifs (sunbursts, geometric designs, and combinations of black and clear glass) are very popular.
- Look for pieces with a good-quality thick body and a high lead content, which allow for deep cutting and a brilliant, lustrous finish.

▼ Vase by Thomas Webb & Sons

This cased vase was designed by Anna Fogelberg and made by Webb for the Rembrandt Guild. Although black and clear glass was a popular Art Deco combination, black glass is rare, and most so-called "black" glass is in fact a very dark "amethyst", as true black is inherently unstable and difficult to produce.

Cocktail shaker by Stuart,
c.1934, ht 22.5cm/8¾in,
$412–577

Vase by Webb, c.1935,
ht 24.5cm/9¾in,
$495–660

Vase by Walsh, c.1935,
ht 25.5cm/10in, **$330–495**

Decanter by
Murray for Royal
Brierley, 1934,
ht 34cm/13¼in,
$1,155–1,485

Vase by Whitefriars, c.1935,
ht 31cm/12in, **$660–990**

▲ Vase by Whitefriars Glassworks

Designed in 1935 and made
until 1937, this hand-blown
vase in "sapphire blue" ("gold
amber" was the other color
frequently used) is a classic
example of one of Whitefriars'
upmarket, one-off pieces.
Although designs by this firm
are unsigned, detailed archive
material and comprehensive
exhibition-catalog records
make attribution possible;
however, misattribution is
becoming increasingly
common following the
enthusiastic response to the
highly successful Whitefriars'
exhibition of 1996/7.

▲ Vase by John Walsh Walsh

The Neo-Georgian cut glass
by this firm was supplemented
by a more innovative selection
of Art Deco glass, of which the
vase above is a good example.
It is decorated with the
"Kendal" pattern – vertical,
shallow-cut "leaf" shapes,
spanned by engraved arched
lines – which was also used on
decanters and tumblers. This
vase, which was made in two
sizes, was designed by W. Clyne
Farquharson, whose signature,
along with the factory name,
appears on the base; later
examples are marked "Tudor".
As a well-documented piece,
this is a good starting-point for
any collector.

▲ Decanter by Murray for Royal Brierley

This hand-blown decanter was
designed by Keith Murray for
Stevens & Williams (known
as "Royal Brierley" after
receiving a royal warrant
from George V). It is an
example of one of Murray's
rare, heavily cut designs. The
horizontal step-cutting was an
extremely difficult and costly
technique, as any flaw in the
glass spelled disaster. Any
Murray piece is highly sought
after and must be attributable
on the basis of a signature,
or from published designs,or
by a written receipt from
a reputable dealer.

▼ Basket by Royal Brierley

The chinoiserie "Willow" pattern featured on this blown-and-cased crystal fruit basket was the hallmark of T.E. Wood, a freelance decorator, who used the design on clear and cased glass. This basket combines a typical Art Deco motif (chinoiserie designs were all the rage during the period) with traditional cutting on the handle, and in this case the combination works well. The "Willow" pattern" is usually found in "blue" ("red" is rare), and is especially sought after by American collectors. The price of this piece reflects both the design's popularity and the higher prices paid for cased glass.

◀ Vase by Harbridge Crystal Co. Ltd

Harbridge Crystal Co. Ltd was a small glass factory about which little is known. Such small firms were to a large degree eclipsed by major makers, although their wares now have the attraction of being very similar in style to those by big names, but far more modestly priced. The vase shown is an odd combination of two different traditions; the naturalistic, curving leaf-cutting is typical of the 1920s and 1930s, but it is rather incongruously topped by traditional miter-cutting around the rim, and there is an equally traditional star-cut foot. However, the piece is well-made, signed, and an interesting example of the marriage of two styles popular in the 1930s.

• Collect by good, bold design rather than name. Many good pieces are unattributable, because small factories did not always mark their pieces.
• Well-documented pieces are a safe starting-point, as they are likely to maintain their prices.
• Cased glass is rarer and more highly priced than uncased glass; large cased examples, in particular, may command a premium.
• Bowls are often lightly scratched, but a piece that scratches easily can be just as easily restored – scratches simply need to be carefully polished away.

Royal Brierley basket, 1930s, ht 20cm/8in, **$990–1,320**

Vase by Harbridge Crystal, 1935, ht 25.5cm/10in, **$66–99**

Other cut glass

European manufacturers were far more willing to embrace the new Art Deco style than their British counterparts. Swedish designers were among the first to exploit the optical effects created by cutting thick, clear glass, and the striking results have a timeless modernity that transcends collecting niches. Some of the long-established French glassmaking companies, such as Baccarat, produced stylish cut-glass pieces that are quintessentially Deco. In Vienna the Lobmeyr glassworks commissioned designs from artists associated with the Wiener Werkstätte ("Vienna Workshops"), among them Josef Hoffmann. Marked pieces by such companies are eagerly sought after, and collectors who are prepared to buy unattributed pieces may well find superb examples at modest prices.

Vase by Orrefors, designed 1932, ht 14.5cm/5¾in, **$330–495**

◀ Vase by Orrefors

This vase, designed by Simon Gate for the Swedish firm of Orrefors, stylishly combines a black foot with a clear crystal body cut in the "1000 Windows" pattern. The effect, similar to that of a hall of mirrors, is obtained by cutting five deep vertical miters and a series of undercut semi-circles into clear glass that is almost 1cm (⅜in) thick. The polished base is marked "OFGA 395/3", identifying the company, the designer, and the pattern. All items attributed to Orrefors should be carefully checked against the firm's detailed design records.

▼ Vase by Orrefors

Another example of Gate's innovative use of the reflective and refractive properties of glass can be seen in this small mold-blown vase. The rows of polished circles (known as "printies") on the thick (1.3cm/½in) glass act as lenses, creating thousands of polished bubbles, which are offset by small mat spots. The design is less well known than "1000 Windows", shown left, and is often overlooked, which makes it correspondingly modestly priced for such a dramatic design. This example is clearly signed "Orrefors Sweden" and marked "GA 1695".

Vase by Orrefors, designed 1937, ht 11.5cm/4½in, **$82–115**

Candelabrum by Baccarat, 1930s, ht 15cm/6in, **$2,475–3,300**

▲ **Candelabrum by Baccarat**
Designed for Baccarat by Jacques Adnet, the cast candelabrum shown above is a wonderful example of French Art Deco at its best. The piece features a silvered bronze base and top, with four geometric cast, then hand-finished, cut-glass arms – a combination of materials that was popularly used in Art Deco lighting design. Such candlesticks are rare and valuable, and few have survived unscathed, as the candles often burnt down into the unprotected glass arms and caused irreparable cracks. A safer compromise was the use of metal candle holders within the glass arms, although this is usually less aesthetically pleasing than all-glass arms. On this example the company name is etched in the bronze base.

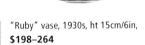

"Ruby" vase, 1930s, ht 15cm/6in, **$198–264**

▲ **"Ruby" vase**
There are several clues to the origins of this unmarked and unidentified hand-blown, cased vase. The slightly pink tone of the "ruby" glass is reminiscent of designs made by glassworks in France or the Val-Saint-Lambert Glasshouse in Belgium, as opposed to the cranberry tone of "ruby" glass made in Britain or Bohemia (now part of the Czech Republic). The highly stylized design suggests that this piece was produced in the 1930s (glass made in the 1920s still had a strong Art Nouveau influence). This piece is a fine example of good design and skilled cutting, and represents excellent value for money.

Bowl by Hoffmann, 1920s, ht 10.5cm/4¼in, **$660–990**

▲ **Bowl by Hoffmann**
This bowl was designed by Josef Hoffmann, a leading Austrian architect and designer and one of the founder members of the Wiener Werkstätte, possibly for the Viennese firm of Lobmeyr. The piece was probably mold-blown and then cut. The thick walls and chunky geometric design are characteristic features of Hoffmann's work.

British engraved glass

In the inter-war years, inexpensive glass made in Czechoslovakia (now the Czech Republic) flooded the lower end of the market, so major British firms such as John Walsh Walsh, Thomas Webb & Sons, and Stevens & Williams concentrated on a range of luxury glass that combined cutting and engraving (a much shallower form of cutting, usually with a copper wheel). There were two major styles of decoration: the first looked back to Art Nouveau and used sinuous flower and plant motifs; the second, influenced by Swedish glassmakers and the new Art Deco style, used more graphic, stylized motifs. Both styles are highly sought after, but pieces that combine or confuse the two are less popular among collectors.

▼ **Vase by John Walsh Walsh**
This art-glass vase was free-blown, allowing the glass blower to control the weight and thickness of the glass to produce the darker foot to represent the water, with the color gradually becoming lighter as the glass becomes thinner toward the rim. It was made in several sizes and colors, including "yellow" and "blue". The decorative motif of water lilies and irises in a pond has been skilfully executed with horizontal cuts for the water, and a classic combination of polished and mat engraving for the irises, the outlines of which have been intaglio cut, acid-polished, and then mat-engraved.

Vase by Walsh, 1930s, ht 25.5cm/10in, **$412–577**

▼ **"Gay glass" bowl by Thomas Webb & Sons**
The luxury "Gay glass" range was launched in 1933. The "Cut Water Lily" pattern shown here was the most sought after of the four different designs in the range, and was used on vases and bowls. The pattern came in four different color schemes: "Spring" (eau-de-nil green), "Evergreen" (dark green), "Sunshine" (a distinctive golden-amber shade made using uranium, and probably the most popular color), and "Crystal" (seen here). This mold-blown example has the acid-etched company mark on the side.

"Gay glass" bowl by Webb, 1933–9, ht 10cm/4in, **$231–264**

"Cactus" vase by Webb, 1935, ht 20cm/8in, **$1,980–2,970**

▲ **"Cactus" vase by Thomas Webb & Sons**
Designed by Anna Fogelberg, this blown clear-glass vase with a stylish black foot offers a complete contrast to the Art Nouveau-influenced bowl shown left. The deeply engraved "cacti" around the base may have been inspired by the vogue for Hollywood Westerns. This design was produced exclusively for the Rembrandt Guild and is very rare; it may even have been a prototype that never went into production because it was too costly to produce or too modern for the more traditional British taste. This piece is marked "Webb Made in England" and "Made Exclusively for Rembrant Guild".

▼ **"Cactus" vase by Murray for Stevens & Williams**
This vase, designed by Keith Murray, would have been hard to produce because of its large size and weight – holding a vase made of such thick glass during the engraving process would have been very arduous. Murray produced a series of cactus designs for this firm, mostly for vases, although two decanters are also known. All examples are very rare; some are unmarked and unsigned. However, the lack of a mark is not problematic, as all Murray designs can be identified from archive material.

"Cactus" vase by Murray for Stevens & Williams, c.1935, ht 38cm/15in, **$3,300–4,950**

▼ **Cocktail shaker by Stuart & Sons Ltd**
Designed by Dame Laura Knight, this Scandinavian-influenced cocktail shaker was one of the pieces shown at an exhibition held at the London department store of Harrods in 1934. All the glass was made by Stuart, which was commissioned by the government to produce tableware designed by top artists in an attempt to promote good glass design. All items shown were marked with the name of the firm and the designer, and are very desirable.

Cocktail shaker by Stuart, 1934, ht 22.5cm/8¾in, **$1,320–1,980**

Other engraved glass

In Sweden many designers worked for both of the two major glassworks – Orrefors and Kosta – thus creating a distinctive Scandinavian style based on both careful placing of engraved decoration, and a clever combination of engraved and clear glass to create depth and perspective. The engraving itself fell into two broad styles, both of which are equally collectable: lyrical engraving, incorporating female figures, landscapes, and flora and fauna; and highly stylized and geometric engraving. In the USA the superb quality of glass by Orrefors and Kosta was matched by Steuben Glassworks, where such notable designers as Sidney Waugh and Walter Dorwin Teague produced Art Deco glass with a strong Scandinavian influence.

Vase by Orrefors, from late 1930s, ht 14cm/5½in, **$495–660**

▲ Vase by Orrefors
This mold-blown engraved vase was designed by Sven Palmqvist, one of the leading contemporary Swedish designers. The engraved decoration of a stylized Art Deco maiden with birds has been produced using a deep, broad copper wheel, and the mat finish contrasts with the polished body. Good condition is important with engraved glass, because surface scratches on the engraving plane cannot be polished off. This vase is signed "Orrefors Palmqvist 2397.C.4.A.R.".

▼ Decanter by Orrefors
Vicke Lindstrand, another major Swedish designer, made this hand-blown decanter for Orrefors, although from c.1950 he worked for Kosta. This piece is a typical Art Deco stylized shape, with a stylish black stopper, and linear engraved graphic decoration of a circus scene. It was originally part of a service that also included six trumpet-bowled glasses in different sizes with black feet. Horses, jugglers, and acrobats are all engraved as simple stylized figures with a combination of broad and shallow lines. Marked "OF.L1132", this is a good example of stylish minimalist Swedish design.

Decanter by Orrefors, 1933, ht 30.5cm/11¾in, **$660–825**

Bowl by Kjellander, 1925–31, ht 11.5cm/4½in, **$198–264**

▲ **Bowl by Kjellander**
Although not produced by a major name or factory, the humor and vitality of this Swedish bowl make it highly collectable. The bowl was thinly blown into a mold and then engraved with stylized cross-country skiers and geometric lines to create a strong sense of movement. The piece bears the signature of Lars Kjellander, who was a designer at Kosta from 1881 until 1925, when he became a freelance glass-engraver.

Vase by Kjellander, 1925–31, ht 17cm/6¾in, **$412–577**

▲ **Vase by Kjellander**
Although this vase, also by Kjellander, is very different in style and treatment from the bowl shown left, the same sense of movement is found in it. Here he has used thicker glass and exploited the optical effects achievable by engraving on both sides. Skilful deep engraving on such areas as the legs make the concave surface appear convex, and the use of random, soft, flowing abrasions and soft mat surfaces gives an added perspective and creates the impression of the wind blowing.

"Agnus Dei vase, c.1935, ht 18.5cm/7in, **$1,320–1,980**

▶ **"Agnus Dei" vase by Steuben Glassworks**
This firm is known for the superb quality of its engraved glass, of which this "Agnus Dei" vase, designed by Sidney Waugh, is a fine example. The stylized mat engraving has a distinctly American Art Deco feel, reminiscent of car mascots and skyscraper decoration. All Steuben pieces are marked, sometimes also with the name of the designer. The value of this vase reflects its status as a major piece by a top firm.

Acid-etched glass

Following early Swedish experiments with acid-etching in the late 18thC, in 1857 the British firm of W.H., B. & J. Richardson patented a technique for fine acid-etched work. A gutta-percha resist was applied to the glass, the design was scratched through it, and the glass then exposed to acid, which ate into the unprotected glass. After World War I, British and French glass makers used acid-etching primarily to eat away the background on art glass. Acid-etched pieces by the French firm of Daum Frères are very sought after; prices and desirability depend on size, complexity, and depth of decoration.

Champagne/cocktail glass by Daum, 1930s, ht 12cm/4¾in, **$495–660** (for a pair)

▶ **Champagne/cocktail glass by Daum Frères**
Acid-etching was a costly technique and was rarely used for tableware. However, it was a popular method of decorating cocktail sets; this hand-blown glass – now one of a pair – was probably one of six. The shallow, acid-etched decoration on the trumpet stem of such high-quality pieces was carried out by hand; on less-exclusive pieces a transfer or template resist might have been used. Drinking glasses are a popular collecting niche, and cocktail glasses in particular have become synonymous with the hedonistic "Jazz" age of the 1920s and 1930s. This glass is signed, as are all pieces by Daum.

▼ **Powder box and cover by Daum Frères**
The ingenious design of this powder box allows the whole top to be lifted off the smooth, rounded base. The powder is stored in a internal container made of clear, undecorated glass that does not detract from the fine, etched, stylized geometric and floral panels of the cover. This piece, which features some hand-finishing on the hand-blown bowl, was originally part of a dressing-table set that would have been very highly priced in the 1930s. With pieces such as this, if the etched surface was too sharp the piece would be redipped in acid to create a smoother polished finish.

Powder box and cover by Daum, 1930s, ht 10cm/4in, **$660–825**

▼ Vase by Daum Frères

On this thinly blown vase, acid-etching has been combined with other techniques to create an extraordinary variety of textures. The pattern has been randomly etched; the glass has been sandblasted to produce a mat surface, and then randomly hand-polished to create a variety of textures. The iceberg-like effect is heightened by the pale blue color. The skilful use of techniques and the large size both contribute to the value; smaller wares would be more affordable. Although this piece is marked "Daum", typically no individual designer is credited.

Bowl by Daum, 1930s, ht 10.5cm/4in, **$2,475–3,300**

▲ Bowl by Daum Frères

Pieces as deeply etched as this hand-blown bowl were very costly to make, and are rare and desirable today. Prolonged exposure to acid would have been needed to create the deeply etched background that contrasts with the bright, hand-polished geometric motifs in relief. The Daum mark is clearly visible on the thick, shiny base.

▼ "Iced" cocktail shaker by Orrefors

The cocktail shaker, an essential part of the Art Deco lifestyle, was introduced to the Orrefors range in the 1920s. This piece is part of the "Iced" series that included ashtrays, bowls, and cocktail glasses. The body was cased in blue and blown into an optic mold, and the cockerel design was protected with a resist before the shaker was plunged into a weak acid to create the "iced" effect. Although most of the firm's pieces bear marks, some from the "Iced" series do not; however, they can be identified from Orrefors catalogs.

Vase by Daum, 1930s, ht 23cm/9in, **$1,155–1,320**

"Iced" cocktail shaker by Orrefors, ht 23cm/9in, **$247–412**

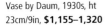

Acid-etched glass ~ 43

French cameo glass

The cameo technique involves fusing two or more layers of glass in various colors, and then hand-carving, acid-etching, or sandblasting the design so that it stands proud of the background. British supremacy in cameo in the 19thC gave way late in that century to French production, with one of the greatest exponents being Emile Gallé. It is possible that Gallé was inspired by the "Portland" vase, a blue-and-white cameo amphora dating from the 1stC BC to the 1stC AD, in London; Gallé in turn inspired the Nancy-based brothers Auguste and Antonin Daum. Production continued in Gallé's workshop after his death in 1904, and in the 1920s and 1930s most pieces (in line with cameo glass in general) were made on an assembly line, using acid-etching. The variety available to collectors is very wide; the maker, size, number of layers, and complexity of the design will determine desirability.

◀ **Vase by Gallé**
Made by and sold through the Gallé workshop in Nancy, this vase is a fine example of a piece with complex cameo decoration. The pale body has been cased in blue glass, which has been etched away at various levels to create an atmospheric landscape and an extraordinary sense of perspective. This piece is signed "Emile Gallé" in script. All Gallé pieces must be signed, but collectors should beware as there is a proliferation of Gallé fakes on the market, most of which bear marks. The best guarantee of authenticity is to buy from a reputable dealer.

Vase by Gallé,
mid-1920s,
ht 19cm/7in,
$2,475–2,970

▼ **Vase by Gallé**
This vase shows one of the rarer color combinations of the 1920s, and the design clearly shows the differing shades achievable using the cameo technique. The dark red of the leaves has been given extra texture by the use of lines for the veins; lighter red shading around the outlines of the leaves creates the impression of added relief, and the pink, or half-red, flowers provide color contrast. Such a vase, signed in relief in cameo on the back, is a good example of middle-range Gallé wares.

Vase by Gallé,
1920s,
ht 9cm/3½in,
$1,650–1,980

Bud vase by Gallé

This bud vase is typical of the many small commercial pieces made by the Gallé workshop. The design is simple compared with the examples shown left, and the colors are more muted, but such an authentic signed Gallé piece is still very desirable. Although muted, the colors on this vase are soft and appealing, whereas those used in reproduction Gallé are harsh approximations. Reproductions made in Eastern Europe should be marked "Tip Gallé"; however, collectors should beware as some unscrupulous vendors remove the "Tip" in order to pass pieces off as originals.

"Elephant" vase by Gallé

This vase shows the rare "blow-out" technique in which multi-layered casing was blown into a mold with an intaglio design (in this case, elephants). The originals remain exceedingly rare, but a new generation of reproductions have been made, clearly marked "Tip Gallé". Many of these are very modestly priced and allow the collector to have an example, albeit a reproduction, of a piece that would be way beyond the average price range.

"Elephant" vase by Gallé, c.1920, ht 38.5cm/15in, **$33,000–49,500**

Vase by Daum Frères

The most skilful cameo workers used up to five layers of color, which demanded great technical expertise because of the different rates at which colors cool. Daum Frères was initially inspired by the Gallé glass exhibited in 1889 in Paris, although most of its landscape cameo vases were produced just after World War I. This superb large example has multiple layers of color, which adds to its value; the pale blue flowers are enameled – a popular Daum feature. The mark near the base is typical.

Vase by Daum,
1920s, ht 23cm/9in,
$4,125–4,950

Bud vase by Gallé,
1920s, ht 10.5cm/4in,
$577–742

Other cameo glass

The firms of Gallé and Daum Frères were by no means the only French makers creating good production-line cameo. Although their pieces command premium prices and are most sought after, many smaller French factories made cameo glass of equal merit but far more modestly priced today. In Sweden, Kosta developed a distinctive stylized one-color cameo range that exploited the high quality of the company's glass, and in Britain, Thomas Webb & Sons and H.G. Richardson & Sons also developed popular cameo lines that combined clear glass with a single color.

▼ **Vase by Richard**
The quality of the small cameo vases made by the Richard glassworks in Lorraine, such as the piece shown here, is on a par with the later industrial Gallé cameo, but is far more modestly priced. The oriental floral design is typical of the factory, as is the use of two bold colors – three-color pieces are rare. Signed in cameo script on the back, this vase represents excellent value for money.

Vase by Richard, 1920s, ht 9cm/3in, **$247–412**

▶ **Vase by Stourbridge Glass Co.**
Pad cameo was a comparatively rarely used technique that involved applying pads of colored glass to a flint body. The clear background was then etched and cut away to leave the colored decoration in higher relief, ready for further carving to provide extra detail. Although unmarked, this vase can be attributed to Stourbridge Glass Co. on the strength of a similar piece, which is marked. Larger, luxury "rock crystal" pad-cameo vases made by Thomas Webb & Sons are worth roughly ten times as much as this little vase.

Vase by Stourbridge, late 1920s, ht 12cm/4in, **$660–990**

"Rich Cameo" vase by
Webb, mid-1930s, ht
19.5cm/7¾in, **$495–660**

"Cameo Fleur" vase by Webb,
1930s, ht 25cm/9¾in, **$495–660**

▲ **"Cameo Fleur" vase by
Thomas Webb & Sons**
This waisted vase was made in
clear glass, overlaid in yellow.
The background was then
etched away to leave the
flowers in relief. Further relief
was achieved by cutting, and
a final acid polish produced a
bright shiny finish. Introduced
in 1931, "Cameo Fleur" vases
were made in various shapes
and colors. The Webb
signature appears in the
cameo decoration on pieces
without feet (such as this
vase), or on the top of the
foot. Chipped feet can pose
a problem, as restoration
may bring the signature
dangerously near to the
edge or even obliterate it.

▲ **"Rich Cameo" vase by
Thomas Webb & Sons**
Thomas Webb & Sons
took over the firm of H.G.
Richardson in 1930, but pieces
in the "Rich Cameo" range still
featured the Richardson mark.
On vases in the range, the
colored decoration is flat,
with indentations for the
detailing on the leaves, and
the clear flint ground is
randomly cut to create
a snakeskin-like
effect. Vases and
bowls were made
in "green",
"blue", "yellow",
"amethyst", and,
rarest and most
desirable, "red".

"Camé" vase, 1935,
ht 18cm/7in, **$660–825**

▼ **"Camé" vase by Kosta**
This vase, part of the "Camé"
range of one-color cameo
(greens and blues were also
used), was probably created
by Tyra Lundgren, a Swedish
designer who lived in Paris
and sent her sketches to Kosta.
The thick, horizontal optic-
ribbing with random lines
creates a watery ground for
the angel fish in relief. Such
cameo pieces were
valuable, exhibition
items – an optic-ribbed
vase with engraved
decoration would be
about a quarter
of the price
of this piece
(marked
"Kosta
1935"
and "Camé
152E").

Enameled glass

Enameling was first used by the Ancient Egyptians, Syrians, and Romans, and was hugely popular in the 16thC and 17thC when it was widely used on drinking glasses. The technique involves painting a mixture of metal oxides and powdered glass onto the surface of a piece, which is then fired to fuse the decoration. In the 1920s and 1930s most glassmaking companies in Britain and continental Europe used enameled freehand or transfer-printed Art Nouveau- and Art Deco-inspired motifs on a wide range of glass. Much sought after are high-quality pieces with decoration by such major designers as Vicke Lindstrand (for Orrefors), members of the Wiener Werkstätte ("Vienna Workshops" – for Lobmeyr), Marcel Goupy, and Auguste-Claude Heiligenstein, who executed many of Goupy's designs for Maison Rouard. More affordable are the stylish tableware pieces produced by a large number of European manufacturers.

◀ Vase by Argy-Rousseau

Although primarily known for his *pâte-de-verre* glass (see pp.30–31), from the mid-1930s Gabriel Argy-Rousseau made a series of rare enameled vases. This blown smoky gray/brown vase has an Egyptian-style frieze of enameled elephants walking along a stylized black path – wild animals were a popular Art Deco motif; the style may well reflect Argy-Rousseau's passion for photography. Such a rare, signed vase will be much sought after.

Vase by Argy-Rousseau, 1930s, ht 15.5cm/6in, $2,475–3,300

▼ Footed bowl by Luce

Jean Luce was the son of a Parisian tableware retailer. In 1931 he opened his own shop, specializing in ceramics and glass. He was a designer rather than maker of glass, and his early designs of the 1920s included enameled decoration, such as the Cubist-inspired geometric floral design shown here, signed with an enameled "JL". Such early enameled pieces are quite rare, as Luce later abandoned the technique as "too bright", concentrating instead on engraving and etching.

Footed bowl by Luce, 1920s, ht 26cm/10¼in, $2,970–3,630

- A combination of good form and good decoration is most desirable, but some everyday forms can be transformed by top-quality polychrome enameled decoration.
- Decoration must be in tip-top condition. Badly abraded enameling will look like a foxed print and should be avoided.
- Pieces with enameled decoration must be treated gently, and cleaned with soft cloths.
- Both handpainted and transfer designs were used; the latter are usually more affordable.

▼ Goblet by Vedart

This unsigned goblet is one of a series thought to have been produced as promotional material by the Venetian glassworks Vedart (short for "Vetri d'Arte"). The goblets were produced in sets of six and in two designs: one decorated with a band of *putti* and the other, more sought after and valuable, the fabulous lady and peacock design shown here. The form of the goblets, which were blown in one size only, is unremarkable; their appeal lies in the superb enameled decoration, which is beautifully shown off in the peacock's tail.

▼ Vase by Vedart

Vedart may well have been a decorating company that bought in glass blanks from other factories, as this vase is another example of a rather mundane form transformed by wonderful, polychrome, freehand-enameled decoration. Here the influence is fashionably oriental, with handpainted branches, blossoms, and insects, and the Vedart signature in enamel. Good condition of the decoration is essential–any damage will drastically reduce the value, as it is impossible to restore enameling successfully.

Vase by Vedart, 1920s, ht 22cm/8in, **$1,650–2,475**

▼ Vase

This unsigned, cut-and-enameled vase was sold through a Paris retailer and is therefore assumed to be French, although it may well have been made elsewhere. Mold-blown, it has vertical sliced cuts and alternate panels transferred with black enamel designs. It is rather large and unusual; cocktail sets of decanters and four matching glasses in the same style are more commonly found.

Goblet by Vedart, 1930s, ht 19.5cm/7½in, **$660–825** (with peacocks), **$495–660** (with *putti*)

Vase, 1930s, ht 18cm/7in, **$660–825**

Perfume bottle atomizer, late 1920s/early 1930s, ht 12cm/4¾in, **$247–330**

▲ **Perfume bottle atomizer**
Small and easy to display, perfume bottles form a popular collecting niche that epitomizes the glamour of the Art Deco period. This mould-blown bottle has a transfer band of enameled roses *en grisaille* (gray), and may well have been a promotional bottle for a rose scent. Although bottles without the atomizer workings are readily found and very inexpensive, they are best avoided, as restoration will be both costly and extremely difficult to carry out successfully.

Vase by Webb Corbett, 1930s, ht 25cm/10in, **$330–495**

▲ **Vase by Webb Corbett Ltd**
Increasing interest is being shown in Webb Corbett glass since a recent exhibition of the company's cut-and-engraved, etched, and enameled pieces, and prices are likely to rise as a result. The blown, footed vase featured above unusually combines acid-etched decoration of stylized pendant motifs with translucent black and blue enamels. The vase, which bears the mark used by the firm in the 1930s, was probably very highly priced at that time, owing to the complexity of the enameling technique.

▼ **Vase by Stuart & Sons**
Enameling could be either painted freehand onto a piece or applied using a combination of transfer-printing (for the outline) and hand-painting, as in the case of the stylized pendant flowers on this large blown vase. This type of glass design, which combined enameling and glass trailing, was introduced by Stuart & Sons in 1931 and produced in various shapes, sizes and designs. The large size and typical Deco color combination make this vase, marked "Stuart England", particularly attractive.

Vase by Stuart, 1930s, ht 31cm/12in, **$495–577**

▼ Candlestick by Stuart & Sons

The enameled decoration on this free-blown candlestick is an unusual example of typical Deco colors and geometric motifs applied to British glass tableware. It is possible that the freehand-painted design was influenced by the phenomenally successful handpainted ceramics designed by Clarice Cliff, and as such the candlestick is very collectible as a single piece – in general, they are much more valuable as pairs. Marked "Stuart Made in England", this candlestick represents the company's middle-range wares – between the vase shown left and the mass-market tableware exemplified by the bowl shown right.

▼ Bowl by Stuart & Sons

The mold-blown bowl featured below, which was available both plain and with patterned decoration, is part of a table service that was one of Stuart's flagship inexpensive, cheerful, modern designer wares. The first colored enameled patterns were introduced by Stuart in 1927, and by 1929 over a third of all new patterns produced by the firm were enameled. This design, by Ludwig Kny (see pp.32–3), was one of the most commonly found. The bowl is marked "Stuart England", together with the number "RD 681309", which refers to the shape rather than the pattern.

• Cocktail sets and vases in stylish Deco patterns tend to be found in two qualities: fine examples in heavy lead glass, with a fine, bright finish, and mass-produced versions (many made in Czechoslovakia – now the Czech Republic) in lighter, thinner glass, typically with a slightly yellow tinge.

• Pieces by less well-known factories are often underrated and undervalued; increasing interest in British Art Deco glass may bring such firms into the front line of collecting, with a corresponding increase in prices.

• Any piece by a less well-known factory or designer must be in perfect condition for top value.

• An unusual mix of enameling with another decorative technique will increase value.

FACT FILE

Bowl by Stuart, 1930s, diam. 20cm/7¾in, **$82–115**

Candlestick by Stuart, 1930s, ht 8cm/3in, **$99–148** (**$240–320** for a pair)

Table glass

In the 1920s and 1930s, Art Deco table-glass production was dominated by Scandinavian glassmakers, particularly those in Sweden. Their distinctive, timeless interpretation of the style, combined with high-quality production, makes such pieces highly attractive to collectors, who can, with patience, build up complete sets. In Britain a few manufacturers produced Art Deco table services; the majority remained committed both to the reproduction Irish-style glass that was popular in the USA and to table services in a Neo-Georgian style. Similarly, most Italian glassmakers produced historical rather than Art Deco table glass. Collectors have a choice of two distinct styles, and can also choose whether to build up complete table services or collect interesting examples of individual pieces.

▼ **Celery vase**

By the late 19thC celery had become such a popular food that many makers produced vases engraved with the word "celery", intended specifically to hold celery sticks. "Celery vase" is now used to describe all footed, short-stemmed, tall, narrow vases made from c.1800. This affordable example is a press-molded, unsigned piece that can be dated to the 1930s by its Deco design, and is a good starting-point for novice collectors.

Celery vase, 1930s, ht 23.5cm/9in, **$33–50**

▶ **Incorporator bottle by Gill**

Incorporator bottles, such as the example by Stan Gill shown right, were used for making vinaigrette. The internal ridges that appear externally as decorative silver bands help the liquid swirl down the bottle, and are a development from the bottles in the shape of the "Michelin Man" that were popular in the Victorian period. The blown stopper on this piece appears cloudy owing to condensation. Usually this would detract from the value, but the rarity, technical skill, and ingenuity of this example, and the affection and esteem in which Gill was held in his native Stourbridge, ensure that it retains its value.

Incorporator bottle by Gill, 1930s, ht 21cm/8in, **$132–198**

"Harlequin" hock glass by Walsh, 1930s, ht 20cm/7¾in, $41–49

Double-ended champagne glass, 1930s, ht 22cm/8½in, $41–49

▲ "Harlequin" hock glass by John Walsh Walsh

This "citron" glass is one of a "Harlequin" set that would have included five other glasses – one each of "green", "pale blue", "dark blue", "ruby", and "amethyst". Walsh glasses were mainly geometrically cut, as shown here, although this example actually bears a fake Webb mark, which was probably added in the 1970s when glass by Thomas Webb & Sons was avidly collected. Unfortunately, this piece also has an area of yellow color missing, where the glass has not been properly dipped.

▲ Double-ended champagne glass

The 1930s debate as to whether champagne should be served in a flute or a saucer was solved by this double-ended champagne glass, which has a slightly iridized finish. It was made in Austria, where such pieces were also known as "marriage" glasses or "wedding" goblets, and came in many intricate designs. Gilt and enameling were common before World War I, but in the 1930s the designs were more subtle. The flat cutting across the tops and bottoms makes them slightly rough to drink from, but they are great fun to collect. Although initially made in sets, these glasses are now mostly found as single items.

Ice bucket, 1930s, ht 13.5cm/5¼in, $99–132 (for a pair without liners) or $198–231 (for a pair with liners)

▲ Ice bucket

This piece, probably orginally one of a pair, was mold-blown, and the "icy" surface decoration was created by fusing crushed glass to the outside surface. Indentations about a third of the way up from the base were designed to hold a metal fretwork liner (often missing), which allowed water from the melting ice to drip through.

Decanter by Stevens & Williams, c.1934, ht 24.5cm/9½in, **$165–247** (unmarked), **$990–1,32 0** (marked), **$412–495** (for a pair)

Teapot by Schott, 1930s, ht 17cm/6¾in, **$330–396**

▲ **Teapot by Schott**

The influence of the Modern Movement can be clearly seen in this glass teapot, which was made in two shapes – the other version was slightly more angular. It was one of the first examples of the lampwork technique being used to produce scientific glass in a design context. A classic example of Bauhaus-inspired glass, this teapot may have been designed by Wilhelm Wagenfeld, who worked for Schott from 1931 until 1935, designing a range of heat-resistant glass household containers that have become 20thC design classics. The example above is marked "Schott Mainz Jena Glass".

Candlestick, 1930s, ht 15cm/6in, **$82–115 ($330–495** for a pair)

▲ **Candlestick**

Made of thin soda glass, with a large folded foot, this candlestick (originally one of a pair) is a good example of the historical designs favored by Italian glassmakers in the 1920s and 1930s. Its wrythen hollow stem and applied handles are clearly inspired by early Venetian glass. Such delicate candlesticks are rare: they often cracked when the candles burnt down into the glass cups, and were also very vulnerable to knocks. Collectors should check carefully for damage, especially to prominent handles.

▲ **Decanter by Stevens & Williams**

Not all Keith Murray's designs for Stevens & Williams were as innovative as his "Cactus" decanter (see pp.38–9). The piece shown above has a very simple form and rather standard decorative band of mat circles, although the black stopper is quintessentially Deco. This piece was part of a complete table service, and appears with a footed tumbler as design 429A in the catalog of Murray patterns. Marked and unmarked examples are known; the latter can be very affordable, as they will only be attributable by reference to archive material, but if one can be matched with a marked decanter, its value will dramatically increase.

▼ Decanter by Orrefors

The simple, elegant design of this blown decanter, with its wrythen stopper and terraced foot, is typical of Scandinavian tableware. This piece was made by Orrefors in the late 1920s, and can be distinguished from similar designs by the British Whitefriars Glassworks by the color (the blue on pieces by Whitefriars is softer) and the terraced foot. Plates, bowls, wine glasses, tumblers, and serving dishes were also produced, and with patience it is possible to build up a complete table service.

▼ Console set by Sinclair Glass Co.

This major American firm is best known for its large, high-quality brilliant-cut glass in Victorian style, and the blown console set shown below, in opaque black-and-white glass with engraved and acid-etched decoration, is a rare example of one of its Art Deco pieces. Such console sets as this are very rarely found complete. On its own, the bowl would be worth about $1,650; pairs of candlesticks are worth three or four times as much as single sticks, and sets of four are even more valuable than pairs.

- With decanters, good condition is essential. Check carefully for internal cracks by holding the piece up to the light – especially important with any engraved examples.
- Stoppers should fit snugly; check that they are not stuck. Bad chips on the peg can be polished out, as can "fritting" (tiny chips).
- Cloudiness, which is caused by condensation, and internal limescale deposit, can also be detected by holding the (empty, dry, and clean) decanter up to the light.

Decanter by Orrefors, 1920s, ht 30.5cm/12in, **$132–198**

Console set by Sinclair, c.1920–23, diam. of bowl 45cm/17½in, ht of candlestick 34cm/13¼in, from **$6,600**

Novelties

The fun-loving 1920s and 1930s were frivolous times. There was a vogue for small glass ornaments, and all the major glass manufacturers developed their own novelty lines. Glass animals were ubiquitous; Austrian, Venetian, and American factories were known for their production of glass flowers, and the Austrian firm of Bimini in Vienna was well known for its lampwork and figural pieces, including some examples featuring nubile female forms. Novelty glass is a collecting niche, where bad taste is better than no taste at all, and the worst possible taste may well prove an excellent investment.

▼ **Hunting goblet by Stevens & Williams**

Hunting goblets were usually produced in sets of six, in a choice of three sizes. The example shown here, made by Stevens & Williams, was one of a set of designs that all featured a small figure in the hollow blown stem. The figures were made by Bill Swingewood, who was known for his highly skilled lampwork. Engraved hunting goblets are rarer and more highly priced than plain ones, but most goblets are good value for money, considering the skill needed to produce them.

Hunting goblet by Stevens & Williams, 1930s, ht 17cm/6¾in, **$165–198**

▶ **"Weasel" vase by Ferro Toso & Co.**

Novelty glass animals were made in prolific quantities by Italian glassmakers. This impressive vase was designed by Guido Balsamo Stella for Ferro Toso & Co., one of the many glassworks based on the island of Murano, near Venice. Known for its Venetian-style vases and goblets, in the late 1920s the company made a range of novelty ornaments in a more typically Art Deco style. This vase, which is made from tiny pieces of blown glass, would have been very difficult to produce and is vulnerable. Such items were usually marked with a paper label (often missing).

"Weasel" vase by Ferro Toso, c.1930, ht 27cm/10½in, **$3,300–4,950**

▼ Ashtray by Thomas Webb & Sons

The Art Deco vogue for travel and glamor is summed up in this handmade ashtray by the Stourbridge-based firm of Thomas Webb & Sons. Made of separate pieces that were assembled when hot, such ashtrays were highly labor-intensive and very vulnerable. The few that have survived must be in tip-top condition for maximum value. This piece is unsigned, but has been identified from company catalogs.

Ashtray by Webb, 1920s, ht 20cm/8in, **$165–247**

Napkin rings by Davidson, 1937, ht 4cm/1½in, **$165–330**

▲ Napkin rings by George Davidson & Co. Ltd

These mold-blown, hand-finished, cut-glass napkin rings, still with their original fake shagreen presentation box, were made as commemorative souvenirs for the coronation of George VI in 1937. George Davidson & Co. Ltd was a major British glassmaker and these napkin rings were probably fairly highly priced in 1937. What is perhaps lacking in aesthetic appeal is more than compensated for by the presence of original packaging (bearing the original silver label, marked "Davidson's Glassware, London, Made in England"), and the commemorative memorabilia interest.

▼ "Verre de soie" basket by Steuben Glassworks

"Verre de soie" was the name used by this American firm for its range of clear glass with a silvery iridescence. The silky sheen made the range very popular and led to a long production run (1905–30). The applied handles on this basket shape (designed by Frederick Carder) are fragile, and the crack at the join is visible. A concealed crack can be detected by gently tapping the glass – a good piece will ring, whereas a cracked example will give a dead sound.

"Verre de soie" basket by Steuben, c.1930, ht 43.5cm/17in, **$1,320–1,980**

Designers, glass makers, & marks

Much art glass made during the 1920s and 1930s is marked. However, some marks can be problematic, either because they are indistinct and difficult to identify, or because they were in the form of a paper label (usually missing). Check the base first, as the mark is often in the center of the bottom of the piece or on the outside edge of the foot. With cameo and enameled glass the mark may be an integral part of the main body. If the mark is not obvious, hold the piece up to the light and turn it in various directions; a soft acid signature often shows up when the glass is held against a piece of black cloth or card. Unmarked pieces have to be identified from company archives.

BRITAIN

Bagley & Co. Ltd
(est. Knottingley, Yorkshire, 1871).
Some glass impressed with date code.

George Davidson & Co. Ltd
(est. Gateshead-on-Tyne, 1867).

Edinburgh & Leith Flint Glass Co.
(est. Leith, c.1864; acquired by Webb's Crystal Glass Co. 1919).

Gray-Stan Glass
(est. London, 1926; closed 1936).
Roughly engraved script signature.

Harbridge Crystal Co. Ltd
(est. Stourbridge, 1928).
Acid-etched signature "HARBRIDGE".

James A. Jobling & Co. Ltd
(est. Sunderland, 1885; from 1921 Jobling & Co; taken over 1975).
Opalescent art glass impressed with registered design number.

John Moncrieff Ltd ("Monart")
(est. Perth, Scotland, 1865).
Paper labels such as the one shown below used 1925 to 1930.

Paper labels such as the one shown below used from 1930 to 1961.

Nazeing Glassworks
(est. London, 1928).
Unmarked; identified by known retailers' labels.

James Powell & Sons Ltd
(est. London, 1834; from 1962 Whitefriars Glassworks; closed 1980).
No marks or signatures; very occasionally original paper labels; identify items from archives.

H.G. Richardson & Sons
(est. Stourbridge, c.1850; taken over c.1930 by Thomas Webb & Sons).
Acid-etched mark of "Richardsons Rich Cameo".

Stevens & Williams
(est. Stourbridge, 1847; from 1930s known as "Royal Brierley").
Wares by Murray for the firm marked from 1934 to 1939 as below.

Stourbridge Glass Co.
(est. Stourbridge, 1922; from 1929 known as Tudor Crystal).

Stuart & Sons Ltd
(est. Stourbridge, 1881).
Wares marked as shown below from 1926 to 1950.

Mark below used from 1930 to 1950.

Stuart
ENGLAND

John Walsh Walsh
(est. Birmingham, 1851; closed c.1951).
Often not marked; occasionally acid-etched "WALSH" or "WALSH" over "ENGLAND".

Thomas Webb & Sons
(est. Stourbridge, 1859).
Mark shown below used c.1906 to 1935.

Webb

Mark below used in the 1930s.

Mark below used c.1935 to 1949.

Webb Corbett Ltd
(est. Stourbridge, 1897 as Thomas Webb & Corbett Ltd; from 1930s Webb Corbett Ltd).
Mark below used c.1930 to 1947.

Whitefriars Glassworks
(see James Powell & Sons Ltd).

CONTINENTAL EUROPE

Argy-Rousseau, Gabriel
(1885–1953).
Marked with a signature in shallow relief.

Baccarat
(est. Baccarat, near Lunéville, 1764).
Many pieces unmarked, as original paper labels are missing; some marked "BACCARAT" in script.

Daum Frères
(est. Nancy, France, 1895).
Mark below wheel-cut on foot rim.

Décorchemont, François-Emile
(1880–1971).

Gallé, Emile (1846–1904)
(Cristalleries d'Emile Gallé, est. Nancy, 1867).
Multiplicity of different marks – refer to specialist books.

Kosta
(est. Smaland, Sweden, 1742).
Cameo pieces engraved "Kosta" on base; designer's name and model number sometimes also included.

Lalique, René (1860–1945).
Various signatures used; all include an "R".

Leerdam
(est. Leerdam, near Rotterdam, 1765; still operating).
Pieces often unsigned and original factory label missing.

Loetz (Johann Loetz-Witwe)
(est. Klostermühle, 1840; closed 1939).
Most pieces unsigned; engraved mark used from 1898.

Luce, Jean (1895–1964).

Marinot, Maurice (1882–1960).
Surname incised in script on base.

Navarre, Henri (1885–1971).
Pieces finely diamond-point engraved "H. NAVARRE" on base.

Orrefors
(est. Orrefors, Sweden, 1898).
Engraved signature "Orrefors"; often includes full name or initials of the designer.

Sabino, Marius-Ernest
(1878–1961; glassworks est. Paris, 1920s).

Schneider, Cristalleries
(est. Epinay-sur-Seine, 1913).
Vases usually signed "Schneider" in script or block capitals.

Val-Saint-Lambert Glasshouse
(est. Seraing-sur-Meuse, near Liège,1825).
Several marks used, often incorporating star-cut design.

Württemberg Metalwork Factory ("WMF")
(est. Geislingen, 1853; glassworks est. Göppingen, 1883).
Mark including the initials "WMF" used from 1914.

Walter, Alméric (1859–1942).
Pieces often signed "A WALTER NANCY".

USA

Steuben Glassworks
(est. New York, 1903, by Frederick Carder; acquired by Corning Glassworks, 1918).

Tiffany, Louis Comfort
(1848–1933)
(Tiffany Glass & Decorating Co. est. Corona, Queens, New York, 1892; closed 1938; Tiffany Studios, est. New York City, 1900).
Tiffany name (signature or initials) and model number typical.

Glossary

acid-etching technique for decorating or reducing ground by using acid to eat away areas unprotected by an acid-resist

acid-polishing process used to give a shiny finish by dipping glass into a mixture of hydrofluoric and sulphuric acid

aventurine from the Italian word for "chance"; decoration of flecked metallic particles

batch the mixture of molten glass in the pot

blowing iron long, hollow metal rod used to inflate the gather of glass

cameo cased glass, with two or more colored layers, with the background carved or acid-etched away to create relief decoration

canes rods of glass drawn by the glass-blower to required thickness for use as decoration

cased pieces made of two or more layers of colored glass or with colored decoration sandwiched between two layers of clear glass

cutting deep cuts, either polished or mat, created by offering the piece to a stone wheel at various angles

diamond-point engraving minutely detailed, fine line decoration using a stiletto-type tool with a sharp diamond point

enameling decorative technique in which colored powdered glass suspended in an oily mixture is painted onto a piece and then fused by heating

engraving lightly abraded mat surface decoration created with a fine copper wheel

flint clear lead or soda glass

gather molten glass on the end of a blowing or pontil iron

hand-blown free-blown glass whose shape is entirely formed through blowing and finishing on the pontil rod

iridescence rainbow-like surface effect created with luster colors or by exposing piece to hot vapors of metal oxides

lampwork glass made from clear or colored rods worked over a blow lamp or torch

lead glass heavy, brilliant glass with a high lead content; rings when struck

"lost-wax" casting technique in which a wax model is cased in plaster and the wax then steamed out ("lost") to make a mold for *pâte-de-cristal* and *pâte-de-verre*; also known as *cire perdue*

lustres metal oxides suspended in an oily material and used for painting onto hot glass

marver metal table used for rolling glass into shape

miter cutting very deep, V-shaped cuts

mold-blowing method of blowing molten glass into a mold to produce both shape and pattern

optic decoration within or on the surface of the glass, which reflects the light in patterns

pâte-de-cristal ("crystal paste") translucent ware made from finely powdered glass paste using "lost-wax" casting

pâte-de-verre ("glass paste") opaque pieces made from crushed glass using the "lost-wax" casting technique

pontil iron solid iron rod used to transfer the blown bubble of glass from the blowing iron for further shaping and/or finishing

pontil mark scar where the pontil iron or rod was removed from the base of a piece

pot crucible in which glass is melted

pressed glass glass with a smooth interior and a molded exterior made by being pressed into a mold by a plunger

prunt blob of glass, in various shapes, applied as decoration

refraction deflection of rays of light from a glass surface

satin glass also known as *verre de soie*; glass with a satin finish

soda glass light, malleable glass with a slightly brownish or greenish tinge; has no lead content and does not ring when struck

star cutting multiple cuts meeting at a central point to create a star effect

studio glass one-off pieces designed and produced by artist-craftsmen

trailing thin threads of glass applied to the surface of a piece

transfer-printing design printed on paper from an engraved copper plate and applied to the surface of a piece

Waldglas ("Forest glass") type of greenish-yellowish glass originally produced in Germany in the Middle Ages

wrythen spiral-twisted ribbed glass

Where to buy

For the new collector, the best place to start buying glass is from a specialist dealer who is a member of one of the antiques associations: NAADA (National Art & Antiques Dealers' Association) and/or AADLA (Art and Antique Dealer's League of America). Most dealers are only too pleased to share their knowledge and experience, provide an opportunity to handle glass, and, most importantly, provide a descriptive receipt. Vetted fairs are also good places to start. Markets and car boot sales are usually best avoided until you have sufficient expertise to distinguish between the masses of glass on show. Similarly, it is probably best only to buy from auction houses once you are more familiar with the area and market values. Although no substitute for actually handling glass, museums offer an opportunity to look at and learn about major glass collections; those listed all have collections that will broaden your visual experience and add to your historical knowledge.

AMERICAN ASSOCIATIONS

National Art & Antiques Dealers' Association (NAADA)
12 East 56th Street
New York NY 10022
USA

Art and Antique Dealer's League of America (AADLA)
353 East 78th Street
New York NY 10021
USA

SPECIALIST DEALERS

Alfies Antiques Market
13–25 Church Street
London NW8 8DT
UK

J. Alastair Duncan Ltd
1435 Lexington Avenue
New York NY 10128
USA

Jeanette Hayhurst
Kensington Church Street
London W8 4HA
UK

Leo Kaplan Ltd
967 Madison Avenue
New York NY 10021
USA

Kensington Church Street Antiques Centre
58–60 Kensington Church Street
London W8 4DB
UK

Lillian Nassau Ltd
220 East 57th Street
New York NY 10022
USA

MAJOR AUCTION HOUSES

Christie's
502 Park Avenue
New York NY 10022
USA

Sotheby's
1334 York Avenue
New York NY 10021
USA

MUSEUMS

Broadfield House Glass Museum
Compton Drive
Kingswinford
West Midlands DY6 9NS
UK

Corning Museum of Glass
One Museum Way
Corning
New York NY 14830
USA

Victoria and Albert Museum
Cromwell Road
South Kensington
London SW7 2RL
UK

What to read

There are many excellent books on glass of this period. The list below gives a selection of general and more specialist books, all of which should be available from either good bookshops or libraries.

GENERAL BOOKS

Arwas, V. Glass: Art Nouveau to Art Deco (London, 1977)

Beard, G. International Modern Glass (London, 1976)

Cummings, K. Techniques of Kiln-Formed Glass (London, 1997)

Dodsworth, R., ed. British Glass Between the Wars (Kingswinford, 1987)

Drahotova, O. European Glass (Prague, 1983)

Janneau, G. Modern Glass (Stourbridge, 1931)

Ploak, A. Modern Glass (London, 1962)

Stennett-Wilson, R. Modern Glass (London, 1975)

SPECIALIST BOOKS

Andrews, F., Clarke, A., and Turner, I. Ysart Glass (London, 1990)

Bacri, Clotilde Daum: Masters of French Decorative Glass (London, 1993)

Baldwin, G.D. Moser Artistic Glass (Ohio, 1997)

Barovier, M. and Doigato, A., eds Animals in Glass (Venice, 1996)

Barovier Mentasti, Rosa Venetian Glass 1890–1980 (Venice, 1992)

Bloch-Dermant, J.G. Argy-Rousseau: Glassware as Art (London, 1991)

Corning Museum of Glass Czechoslovakian Glass 1350–1980 (New York, 1981)

Deboni, F. and Klein, D. Venini Glass (Verona, c.1996)

Duncan, A. Orrefors Glass (Woodbridge, 1995)

Duncan, A. and De Bartha, G. Glass by Gallé (London, 1984)

Evans, W., Ross, C., and Werner, A. Whitefriars Glass: James Powell & Sons of London (London, 1985)

Forsythe, R.A. Made in Czechoslovakia (Ohio, 1982)

Gardner, P.V. Frederick Carder: Portrait of a Glassmaker (New York, 1985)

Jackson, L., ed. Whitefriars Glass: The Art of James Powell & Sons (Shepton Beauchamp, 1996)

Opie, J. Scandinavian Ceramics and Glass in the 20th Century (London, 1989)

Osteergard, D. and Strizler-Levine, N., eds The Brilliance of Swedish Glass 1918–1939 (Yale, 1996)

Petrova, S. and Olvie, J.-L. Bohemian Glass 1400–1989 (New York, 1990)

Ricke, H. and T., eds Swedish Glass Factories, Production Catalogs 1915–1960 (Munich, 1987)

Index

Acknowledgements
All pictures photgra... ...Ltd, courtesy of Jeanette
Hayhurst, except:
31tc Christie's Ima... ...23tc, 23br Haworth Art
Gallery, Accrington... ...46tr, 47tl, 47tc,
50tc, 50br, 51bl,... ...W1Y OBS; 37tc
Octopus Publishin... ...arket, 1–7 Davies
Mews, London W1... ...nd 302, Grays Antique
Market, 58 Davies... ...ey/Trio, stand L24,
Grays Mews Antiq... ...30l, 30r, 31l,
45bc, 48l, 48r, !... ...nner/Jeanette Hayhurst.
Jacket photogra...